FOLEGAN

Travel Guide

Your Ultimate Insider's Companion to Greece's Untouched Cycladic Gem: Discover Hidden Beaches, Authentic Culture, Sustainable Adventures, and Perfect Itineraries for Every Traveler

James J. Lambert

Copyright Page

© 2025

All rights reserved.

This book, including all its contents, is protected by copyright law and may not be reproduced, distributed, or transmitted in any form or by any means whether electronic, mechanical, photocopying, recording, or otherwise without the prior written permission of the copyright holder, except as permitted by applicable copyright law. Unauthorized use or reproduction of this work is strictly prohibited and may result in legal action. For permissions or inquiries, please contact the author or their representative. All rights, including those not expressly granted, are reserved.

Disclaimer

The information in this book is for general informational and entertainment purposes only. While every effort has been made to ensure accuracy, the author and publisher make no warranties, express or implied, regarding the completeness, reliability, or suitability of the content. Readers are encouraged to verify details independently before making travel plans or decisions.

The author and publisher are not responsible for any loss, injury, or inconvenience resulting from the use of this book. Any reliance on the information provided is strictly at the reader's own risk. Views expressed are those of the author and do not constitute professional advice.

TABLE OF CONTENTS

CHAPTER 1: WELCOME TO FOLEGANDROS —— 11

1.1 Introduction to the Island —— 11
1.2 Why Folegandros? (Charming, Underrated & Authentic) —— 12
1.3 Quick Facts & Historical Snapshot —— 13
1.4 Who This Guide Is For (Tailored Travel Styles) —— 14
1.5 How to Use This Book Effectively —— 15

CHAPTER 2: ESSENTIAL TRAVEL PLANNING —— 18

2.1 Entry Requirements (Passports, Visas & Vaccinations) —— 18
2.2 When to Visit: Seasonal Overview & Weather Tips —— 20
2.3 How Long to Stay: Trip Duration by Interest —— 21
2.4 What to Pack for Island Life (By Season & Activity) —— 22
2.5 Accessibility Tips (For Families, Seniors & Travelers with Disabilities) —— 24

CHAPTER 3: GETTING TO AND AROUND FOLEGANDROS —— 27

3.1 How to Get to Folegandros —— 27
3.2 Island Transportation —— 30
3.3 Navigating Chora and Other Villages —— 33

CHAPTER 4: WHERE TO STAY IN FOLEGANDROS —— 36

4.1 Overview of Island Villages & Best Areas to Stay —— 36
4.2 Budget-Friendly Stays: Hostels, Studios & Guesthouses —— 38
4.3 Mid-Range & Boutique Hotels —— 39
4.4 Luxury Villas, Spa Hotels & Cliffside Resorts —— 40
4.5 Unique & Sustainable Stays (Eco-Lodges, Airbnb Gems) —— 42

CHAPTER 5: TOP ATTRACTIONS & MUST-SEES - THE ESSENTIAL FOLEGANDROS EXPERIENCE --- 44

- 5.1 Chora: The Cliffside Capital --- 44
- 5.2 Panagia Church & the Scenic Hike --- 45
- 5.3 Kastro Village & Historical Walks --- 47
- 5.4 Agali Beach & the Coastal Trails --- 48
- 5.5 Sunset Viewpoints & Iconic Landscapes --- 49

CHAPTER 6: HIDDEN GEMS & LOCAL SECRETS - WHERE FOLEGANDROS TRULY REVEALS ITS SOUL --- 51

- 6.1 Remote Beaches: Livadaki, Vardia & Agios Nikolaos --- 51
- 6.2 Untouched Villages & Lesser-Known Paths --- 53
- 6.3 Authentic Local Experiences: Ceramics, Honey, and Raki --- 55
- 6.4 Under-the-Radar Dining & Sunset Spots --- 56

CHAPTER 7: FLAVORS OF FOLEGANDROS – FOOD & DRINK --- 58

- 7.1 Must-Try Local Dishes --- 58
- 7.2 Top Taverns, Family-Run Eateries & Beachside Grills --- 60
- 7.3 Wine Bars, Cafés & Cocktails with a View --- 61
- 7.4 Food Markets & Culinary Tours --- 63

CHAPTER 8: SHOPPING & ISLAND FINDS – TREASURES OF FOLEGANDROS --- 66

- 8.1 Souvenir Ideas & Where to Buy Them --- 66
- 8.2 Handmade Crafts, Jewelry & Local Art --- 68
- 8.3 Where to Shop on a Budget --- 70
- 8.4 High-End Boutiques & Artisan Studios --- 71

CHAPTER 9: OUTDOOR ADVENTURES – EMBRACING FOLEGANDROS' WILD BEAUTY --- 73

    9.1 HIKING ROUTES WITH STUNNING SEA VIEWS -- 74

    9.2 SNORKELING & SWIMMING IN HIDDEN COVES --- 76

    9.3 BOAT TOURS, ISLAND HOPPING & SEA CAVES -- 77

    9.4 YOGA, WELLNESS & NATURE IMMERSION -- 79

CHAPTER 10: CULTURE, TRADITIONS & LOCAL LIFE - EMBRACING THE HEARTBEAT OF FOLEGANDROS -- 82

    10.1 CULTURAL ETIQUETTE & ISLAND WAY OF LIFE --- 83

    10.2 RELIGIOUS FESTIVALS & LOCAL CELEBRATIONS --- 84

    10.3 ISLAND MUSIC, DANCE & FOLK TALES --- 86

    10.4 MUSEUMS, CHURCHES & HISTORICAL HIGHLIGHTS -- 88

CHAPTER 11: SEASONAL TRAVEL GUIDE - DISCOVERING FOLEGANDROS THROUGH THE YEAR --- 90

    11.1 VISITING IN SPRING: WILDFLOWERS & SERENITY -- 90

    11.2 SUMMER ON THE ISLAND: FESTIVITIES & WARM WATERS ---------------------------------- 92

    11.3 AUTUMN ESCAPES: QUIET SHORES & CULINARY DELIGHTS -------------------------------- 94

    11.4 WINTER IN FOLEGANDROS: PEACEFUL, SLOW, AND AUTHENTIC ---------------------------- 95

CHAPTER 12: CURATED ITINERARIES - EXPLORING FOLEGANDROS ONE PERFECT DAY AT A TIME -- 98

    12.1 ONE-DAY HIGHLIGHTS TOUR --- 98

    12.2 CLASSIC 3-DAY GETAWAY -- 100

    12.3 ULTIMATE 7-DAY ISLAND IMMERSION --- 101

    12.4 FAMILY ADVENTURE ITINERARY -- 102

    12.5 ROMANTIC ESCAPE FOR COUPLES --- 102

    12.6 BUDGET EXPLORER'S PLAN --- 103

    12.7 EXCLUSIVE LUXURY EXPERIENCE --- 104

CHAPTER 13: ISLAND HOPPING & EXCURSIONS - ADVENTURES BEYOND THE HORIZON ---- 106

13.1 Day Trips to Milos, Santorini & Sikinos ---- 106
13.2 Boat Excursions Around Folegandros ---- 108
13.3 Scenic Picnics & Off-the-Grid Spots ---- 110

CHAPTER 14: NIGHTLIFE & AFTER DARK - THE SOUL OF FOLEGANDROS AT TWILIGHT ---- 113

14.1 Sunset Bars & Rooftop Lounges ---- 113
14.2 Live Music & Cultural Nights ---- 115
14.3 Stargazing & Quiet Evenings in Nature ---- 117

CHAPTER 15: TRAVEL TIPS & SAFETY - NAVIGATING FOLEGANDROS WITH CONFIDENCE ---- 120

15.1 Local Laws & Traveler Rights ---- 120
15.2 Avoiding Common Pitfalls & Scams ---- 122
15.3 Emergency Numbers & Medical Access ---- 123
15.4 Health, Safety & Solo Travel Considerations ---- 124
15.5 Travel Apps & Useful Services ---- 126

CHAPTER 16: MANAGING YOUR BUDGET - EXPLORING FOLEGANDROS WITHOUT BREAKING THE BANK ---- 128

16.1 Currency, ATMs & Card Use ---- 128
16.2 Daily Costs & Typical Prices ---- 130
16.3 Budgeting Tips for Every Traveler ---- 131
16.4 Free & Low-Cost Experiences ---- 133

CHAPTER 17: INDULGENT ESCAPES – LUXURY TRAVEL IN FOLEGANDROS --- 135

17.1 5-Star Hotels with Infinity Pools --- 135

17.2 Private Yacht Charters & Helicopter Transfers ------------------------------ 137

17.3 Fine Dining & Premium Wine Tastings --- 138

17.4 Spa Days & Private Retreats -- 139

CHAPTER 18: GUIDE FOR SOLO TRAVELERS --- 141

18.1 Is Folegandros Safe for Solo Travel? --- 142

18.2 Solo-Friendly Activities & Social Hotspots -------------------------------------- 143

18.3 Meeting Locals & Other Travelers -- 144

CHAPTER 19: FAMILY-FRIENDLY TRAVEL -- 148

19.1 Things to Do with Kids --- 148

19.2 Best Family Accommodations--- 150

19.3 Child-Friendly Beaches & Attractions --------------------------------------- 151

19.4 Practical Tips for Traveling with Children --------------------------------------- 152

CHAPTER 20: RESPONSIBLE TRAVEL IN FOLEGANDROS ---------------------------- 155

20.1 How to Travel Sustainably --- 155

20.2 Eco-Friendly Tours & Lodging --- 157

20.3 Respecting Local Culture & Communities ------------------------------------ 158

20.4 Waste Management & Water Use Tips --- 159

CHAPTER 21: FOR THE INSTAGRAMMER & PHOTOGRAPHER -------------------- 162

21.1 Most Photogenic Spots on the Island --- 162

21.2 Best Time of Day for Lighting & Crowds ------------------------------------- 164

21.3 Local Photographers & Workshops --- 165

21.4 Top Hashtags & Social Media Tips --- 166

CHAPTER 22: WHAT NOT TO DO IN FOLEGANDROS ------------------------------ 169

22.1 COMMON MISTAKES FIRST-TIME VISITORS MAKE --- 169

22.2 WHAT'S CONSIDERED RUDE OR TABOO --- 171

22.3 OVERHYPED SPOTS VS. GENUINE EXPERIENCES --- 172

22.4 WEATHER HAZARDS & TRAVEL MISCALCULATIONS --- 173

CHAPTER 23: FINAL DEPARTURE TIPS --- 175

23.1 HOW TO GET BACK (FERRIES, TRANSFERS, FLIGHTS) --- 175

23.2 LAST-MINUTE GIFT & SOUVENIR GUIDE --- 177

23.3 ENDING YOUR TRIP GRACEFULLY: WHAT TO REMEMBER --- 178

CHAPTER 24: APPENDICES & BONUS RESOURCES --- 181

24.1 ESSENTIAL GREEK PHRASES FOR TRAVELERS --- 181

24.2 TRAVEL RESOURCES: SITES, BOOKS & BLOGS --- 182

24.3 CONTACT INFO: TOURISM OFFICE, POLICE, HOSPITALS --- 184

24.4 IMPORTANT ADDRESSES & GPS LINKS --- 185

24.5 FESTIVAL CALENDAR & LOCAL EVENTS --- 186

24.6 PACKING CHECKLIST TRAVEL JOURNAL PAGES --- 187

24.7 LOCAL FERRY SCHEDULES & TRANSPORTATION CONTACTS --- 188

General map of Folegandros

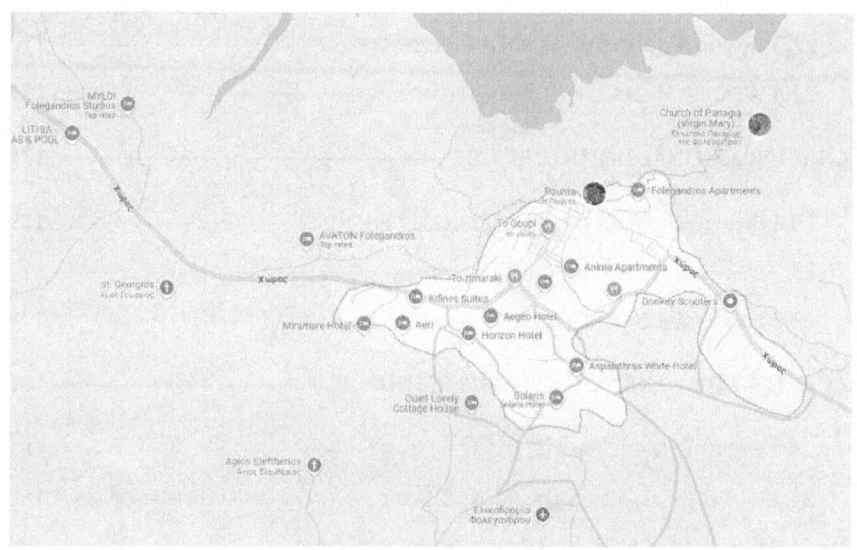

https://maps.app.goo.gl/m8U6hSMCDRLZox44A

Scan the QR-Code to see the real-time location.

Chapter 1: Welcome to Folegandros

1.1 Introduction to the Island

The first time I set foot on Folegandros, I arrived by ferry as the sun began to dip beneath the horizon, casting a honey-gold glow across the cliffs that seem to rise straight out of the sea. It felt like stepping into a dream, no high-rise hotels, no noisy tourist traps, just a sense of calm and authenticity that is all too rare in today's travel world. Nestled between Santorini and Milos, this little Cycladic gem has somehow managed to keep itself just under the radar. And that's precisely its charm.

Folegandros is a place where time stretches out. Life slows down to the rhythm of waves lapping against white-washed harbor walls. The island's heart beats not in its sights alone, but in the unhurried conversations over glasses of rakomelo, in the timeless rhythm of goats clattering across sunbaked paths, and in the wind that whispers through the narrow alleyways of its cliff-hugging Chora. It's not just a destination, it's an invitation to exhale.

1.2 Why Folegandros? (Charming, Underrated & Authentic)

So why Folegandros, you might ask, when you could be sipping cocktails in Santorini or diving into Mykonos nightlife? Well, that's exactly the point. Folegandros offers something altogether different. It's the kind of place where your days are not dictated by a packed itinerary but by your instincts. Wake with the sun, wander through sleepy villages, stumble upon a hidden taverna, and let the day unfold like a story.

This island is for the traveler, not the tourist. It's a haven for those who seek:

- **Authenticity**: Villages like Ano Meria are still dotted with "themonies," traditional farmhouses preserved in time. Locals bake bread in stone ovens, and donkeys are still used to carry goods.

- **Peace**: With no airport and limited ferry connections, the island remains blissfully untouched by mass tourism.

- **Unspoiled Beauty**: The rugged coastline is punctuated by secluded beaches, and the dramatic cliffs rival those of Santorini, without the crowds.

- **Intimate Experiences**: Everything here is scaled for serenity, family-run guesthouses, cozy tavernas, and walks that make you feel like you're discovering a forgotten corner of the world.

This is a place to disconnect from the noise and reconnect with yourself.

1.3 Quick Facts & Historical Snapshot

Before we go any further, let's get our bearings.

Quick Facts:

- **Location**: Southern Cyclades, Aegean Sea
- **Size**: Approx. 32 square kilometers
- **Population**: Just over 750 permanent residents
- **Main Settlements**: Chora, Karavostasis (port), Ano Meria
- **Currency**: Euro (€)
- **Language**: Greek (though many speak English in tourist-facing areas)

A Touch of History

Folegandros has been inhabited since ancient times, with roots tracing back to the Dorians in the 8th century BC.

Its strategic location made it a target for pirates and conquerors over the centuries, including the Venetians and Ottomans. Yet through it all, Folegandros maintained a strong sense of independence and cultural identity. Even during more recent periods, such as the early 20th century, the island served as a place of political exile, lending it a layer of quiet resilience that's still felt in its windswept hills and stoic architecture.

The island's architectural crown jewel, the Kastro of Chora, dates back to the 13th century and still houses local families. It's a living monument, an unembellished echo of a time when villages were built like fortresses to fend off raiders.

1.4 Who This Guide Is For (Tailored Travel Styles)

Whether you're a wide-eyed wanderer seeking solitude or a discerning traveler chasing underexplored gems, Folegandros speaks many languages. I've crafted this guide with all types of travelers in mind:

- **Solo Travelers**: If you're traveling alone, you'll find peace in the island's quiet trails and connection in its friendly tavernas.

- **Couples**: There's a reason many honeymooners come here: the sunsets, the walks along the cliff's edge, the candlelit dinners in the Chora.

- **Families**: While there's not a theme park in sight, kids can roam freely in car-free villages, splash in shallow coves, and learn a slower way of life.

- **Budget Travelers**: Avoiding the tourist circus means lower prices. Stay in a traditional guesthouse, eat fresh souvlaki, and enjoy the island's riches without breaking the bank.

- **Luxury Seekers**: Think understated elegance, boutique hotels with infinity pools gazing into the Aegean and curated dining under the stars.

Each chapter that follows is color-coded for ease, with notes and recommendations specific to these traveler types. Whether you're hiking solo to the remote Agios Georgios beach or splurging on a cliffside suite in Chora, this book has you covered.

1.5 How to Use This Book Effectively

I've organized this guide with the belief that travel should be both spontaneous and informed. You'll find detailed breakdowns of logistics, suggested itineraries, and cultural insights that go beyond the surface.

Here's how to make the most of it:

- **Start with Chapter 2** to plan your trip efficiently. It covers the nuts and bolts, when to go, what to pack, and how to get there.

- **Flip to Chapter 5** if you're itching to see the island's highlights, the postcard moments, and must-visit landmarks.

- **Crave authenticity?** Chapter 6 will take you off the beaten path.

- **Culinary enthusiast?** Chapter 7 is your ticket to the island's vibrant food culture.

- **Pressed for time?** Chapter 12 lays out flexible itineraries, from whirlwind 24-hour escapades to relaxed week-long adventures.

- **Need real-time help?** Chapter 24 compiles essential contacts, local resources, and handy Greek phrases to help you navigate with ease.

Each section includes personal insights, seasonal tips, and hidden treasures I've uncovered during my own time on the island. From the best time to hike to the Church of Panagia, to the lesser-known bakery that makes melt-in-your-mouth amygdalota (almond cookies), you'll find the kind of advice that only comes from being there.

A Personal Invitation

As you begin this journey, I invite you to do more than just visit Folegandros, immerse yourself. Talk to the locals. Let your days be shaped by serendipity. Watch the stars from your terrace in silence. Hike not for the destination, but for the rhythm of your breath. And above all, let go of any pressure to do it all, because on Folegandros, doing less is doing it right.

Let this book be your companion, your planner, and your window into a world where time stands still and beauty whispers, rather than shouts.

Welcome to Folegandros. The journey begins here.

Chapter 2: Essential Travel Planning

Everything You Need to Know Before Arriving in Folegandros

Before you can wander Folegandros' wind-kissed trails or sip ouzo beneath a blooming bougainvillea in Chora, a little planning goes a long way. This island may be remote by design, but getting here and getting the most out of your stay is refreshingly simple with the right preparation. I've been coming to Folegandros for over a decade, and with each trip, I learn something new. Consider this your go-to planning compass, a prelude to your sun-drenched adventure.

2.1 Entry Requirements (Passports, Visas & Vaccinations)

Let's start with the essentials. You don't want paperwork standing between you and paradise.

Passports:

Travelers from most countries, including the US, UK, Canada, Australia, and the EU, must present a valid passport with at least six months' validity from the date of entry. This rule is rarely enforced strictly in Greece, but border agents can and occasionally do check, especially at ferry ports and airports.

Visas:

- EU citizens can travel freely to Greece without a visa.

- US, Canadian, UK, and Australian passport holders can visit for up to 90 days within 180 days without a visa (part of the Schengen Zone agreement).

- For longer stays or multiple European visits, check your Schengen balance and consider applying for a long-stay visa if needed.

Vaccinations:

There are no mandatory vaccinations to enter Greece. However, I recommend:

- Staying up to date on routine vaccines (MMR, Tetanus, Polio)

- Hepatitis A: advisable if you plan to eat local foods or explore rural areas

- Travel insurance that covers health and evacuation is a wise investment, as medical facilities on Folegandros are limited to a local clinic.

2.2 When to Visit: Seasonal Overview & Weather Tips

Folegandros wears a different charm each season, and knowing when to visit can transform a good trip into an unforgettable one.

Spring (April – early June):
This is my favorite time. The hills are alive with wildflowers, the hiking trails are bathed in golden light, and temperatures are warm but not scorching (18–25°C / 64–77°F). Tourism is just beginning to stir, meaning you'll share the island with locals and the occasional savvy traveler.

Summer (Mid-June – August):
This is high season. The island pulses with energy, from beach parties in Agali to music events in Chora. Expect long sunny days (28–35°C / 82–95°F), lively tavernas, and full bookings. If you're visiting in July or August:

- Book accommodation and ferries in advance

- Prepare for stronger Meltemi winds, especially in late July

- Escape the midday heat with a long lunch or a nap, local style

Autumn (September – October):
A second sweet spot. The sea is warm from summer's kiss, and the crowds begin to thin.

Prices dip, sunsets are magical, and the vibe is relaxed yet still vibrant. Ideal for romantic escapes and leisurely exploration.

Winter (November – March):
The island retreats into itself. While ferries still run, services are minimal, many businesses shut down, and the weather turns unpredictable (cooler days, occasional storms). However, if solitude is your luxury, this might be your moment.

2.3 How Long to Stay: Trip Duration by Interest

Folegandros may be small, but its depth is surprising. How long should you stay? Let your interests guide you.

Quick Escape (2–3 days):
Perfect for:

- Island-hopping travelers seeking a calm interlude
- Visitors from Santorini looking for authenticity

Must-dos:

- Wander Chora and the Kastro
- Hike to the Church of Panagia
- Swim at Agios Nikolaos beach

Leisure Lover's Stay (4–5 days):

Ideal for those wanting a balance of rest and discovery. You'll have time to:

- Explore Ano Meria's Ecological and Folklore Museum
- Take day hikes to Livadaki or Ambeli Beach
- Enjoy long, lazy lunches at seaside tavernas

Immersive Retreat (7+ days):

The sweet spot for a deep connection with the island. Perfect for:

- Artists, writers, or remote workers
- Slow travelers soaking in every sunset

Activities to add:

- Cooking classes or foraging walks with locals
- Explore hidden trails, like Petousis Gorge
- Day trip to Sikinos or Milos via ferry

2.4 What to Pack for Island Life (By Season & Activity)

Packing for Folegandros is about striking a balance between practicality and ease. The island's laid-back charm means there's no need for high fashion, but don't underestimate the elements.

All Seasons Essentials:

- Sturdy walking shoes or sandals (for cobblestones and hikes)
- Sunscreen, sunglasses & a wide-brimmed hat
- Swimwear (bring two, there's always a chance for a spontaneous dip)
- Light scarf or shawl (for sun protection or breezy evenings)
- Refillable water bottle (eco-conscious and necessary for hikes)

Seasonal Must-Haves:

Spring & Autumn:

- Lightweight layers (mornings and evenings can be cool)
- Light rain jacket (just in case)
- Bug spray (mosquitoes can surprise you near still water)

Summer:

- Breathable, UV-protective clothing
- After-sun gel or aloe vera
- Flip-flops or water shoes for rocky beaches

Winter:

- Warm layers and a windproof jacket
- Books, journals, or indoor entertainment
- Closed-toe shoes (some trails get muddy)

For Photographers & Creatives:

- Portable tripod (especially for sunset shots in Chora)
- Drone (allowed in non-restricted areas, stunning aerials await)

2.5 Accessibility Tips (For Families, Seniors & Travelers with Disabilities)

Folegandros is a traditional island, which means modern infrastructure hasn't caught up everywhere. That said, thoughtful planning can help every traveler enjoy the island comfortably.

For Families:

- Chora is car-free, making it safe for kids to roam
- Many beaches are accessible only by boat or hike; bring a baby carrier, not a stroller
- Taverns are family-friendly; don't hesitate to ask for kid-friendly meals

For Seniors:

- Stick to central accommodations in Chora or Karavostasis to reduce uphill walking
- Some boutique hotels offer shuttle services or in-town transfers
- Ask your host for the easiest beach access points. Agali and Vardia are good options

For Travelers with Disabilities:

- The island's narrow alleys and steep terrain can be challenging
- Choose hotels with ground-level rooms or minimal steps (some cliffside properties are not accessible)
- Boat trips to beaches often require stepping between docks. Ask the captains in advance about mobility assistance
- Medical care is available at the local clinic; serious emergencies require evacuation to Santorini or Athens

Prepare, Then Let Go

Folegandros rewards those who plan, but it enchants those who let go. Prepare well, yes. But leave space in your suitcase for spontaneity and in your schedule for moments that move you.

Let the sun decide your pace. Let the scent of oregano and thyme guide your wanderings. And above all, pack your curiosity, it will serve you better than any map.

In the next chapter, we'll dive into Getting There & Getting Around, because this hidden gem may be remote, but reaching it is part of the magic.

Chapter 3: Getting to and Around Folegandros

Every time I arrive on Folegandros, there's a moment, right as the ferry rounds the final bend and the whitewashed houses of Karavostasis come into view, when I feel like I've returned to a secret world. It's not the easiest island to reach, and that's precisely what makes it so rewarding. This isn't Santorini or Mykonos, where airports hum with crowds and taxis jostle for position. Folegandros asks for a little effort, but it gives you solitude, soulfulness, and the rare luxury of unspoiled beauty.

In this chapter, I'll walk you through how to get to Folegandros, how best to travel across the island, and how to navigate its charming towns and trails. Whether you're arriving with a backpack or a suitcase on wheels, this is everything you need to know about getting to and around this Cycladic gem.

3.1 How to Get to Folegandros

(Flights to Nearby Islands & Ferry Options)

Folegandros doesn't have an airport, and that's one of its great blessings.

This small fact filters out the crowds and makes arrival feel like an earned treasure. But don't worry, getting here isn't complicated; you just need to know your options.

Nearest Airports

The closest airports to Folegandros are:

- **Santorini (JTR):** The most popular entry point, with frequent international and domestic flights. From Santorini, Folegandros is just a 45-minute fast ferry or a 2-hour regular ferry away.

- **Milos (MLO):** A smaller, quieter alternative. Flights from Athens are short and scenic. The ferry from Milos to Folegandros takes 1–2 hours, depending on the boat.

If you're flying into Athens, consider a direct domestic flight to Santorini or Milos, then continue by sea. Booking in advance, especially in summer, is essential. I recommend checking Sky Express and Olympic Air for domestic flight schedules.

Ferry Connections

Once in the Cyclades, the ferry system is your bridge to Folegandros.

- **From Santorini:**
    - High-speed ferries (SeaJets or Golden Star) run daily in high season (April–October).
    - Book early in July and August, as these routes fill fast.

- **From Milos:**
    - Slower but less crowded.
    - Perfect for those doing an island-hopping itinerary off the beaten path.

- **From Athens (Piraeus Port):**
    - A longer journey: 7–10 hours, depending on stops.
    - Overnight ferries offer cabins for comfort, great if you're not in a rush.

Insider Tips:

- Use Ferryhopper or DirectFerries to check schedules, compare vessels, and book tickets.
- Arrive at ferry ports at least 30–45 minutes early, boarding can be hectic, especially at large ports like Piraeus or Santorini.

- Keep ferry tickets on your phone or printed, as reception can be spotty at sea.

3.2 Island Transportation

(Scooters, Buses, Cars & Walking Routes)

Once you've landed on Folegandros, the good news is: you don't need much to get around. The island is compact (just 13 km long), and most attractions are within easy reach.

Scooters & ATVs

If you're comfortable on two wheels, this is the best way to explore the island. Winding roads, sparse traffic, and spectacular views make every ride memorable.

- Rentals are available in Karavostasis and Chora.
- Prices start at around €20–30/day for scooters and €40–50/day for ATVs.
- Bring your driver's license and an International Driving Permit (IDP); most agencies require it.

Pros:

- Flexibility to reach remote beaches like Livadaki or Ambeli
- Easy parking in tight village streets

- Fun and breezy, especially in the warm season

Rental Cars

Ideal for families or those less confident on two wheels.

- Several agencies offer compact cars and 4x4s.
- Summer rentals start at €50–70/day.
- Roads are well-paved, but narrow. Take it slow, especially around sharp turns.

Tip: Book early in July–August, rental options sell out quickly.

Public Buses

Simple, affordable, and surprisingly efficient.

- Buses connect Chora, Ano Meria, Agali, and Karavostasis.
- In summer, buses run hourly during peak times, but much less frequently off-season.
- Tickets are €2–3, paid onboard or at local kiosks.

Great for:

- Budget travelers
- Short hops between major villages
- Avoiding parking hassles in Chora

Walking & Hiking

Folegandros is a walker's paradise. Trails crisscross the island, often offering stunning views of sea cliffs and silent valleys.

- Many beaches (like Katergo) are accessible only on foot or by boat.
- Wear good walking shoes, as paths are often rocky and sun-exposed.
- Start early in summer to avoid the heat, and carry water at all times.

Some favorite walking routes:

- **Chora to Panagia Church:** A zigzag path with sunset views that will take your breath away.
- **From Ano Meria to Agios Georgios Beach:** A rugged path with pastoral scenery and a sleepy, secluded shore.

3.3 Navigating Chora and Other Villages

(Maps & Travel Apps)

If you've ever longed to get lost in a Greek island village, Chora will grant that wish, but gently.

The car-free labyrinth of whitewashed alleyways and hidden courtyards can be bewildering at first, but part of the charm is stumbling upon quiet corners, artisan boutiques, or a kafeneio serving chilled raki.

Getting Around Chora

- No vehicles allowed: walk everywhere.
- Most paths are stone-paved and safe, but wear comfortable shoes, heels don't belong here.
- In the heat of the day, find shady spots under pergolas or at small churches.

Must-visit corners:

- **Pounta Square**: Great for people-watching over a freddo espresso.
- **Kastro District**: A medieval enclave with narrow, photogenic passages.

- **Panagia Church Trail**: Begins from Chora and leads to the island's most iconic viewpoint.

Ano Meria

This farming village is wonderfully authentic. Visit the Folklore Museum, then enjoy lunch at Irini's Tavern, where the matriarch still makes pies by hand.

- The village stretches linearly along the main road.
- Few signs, so Google Maps or Maps.me are helpful for pinpointing trailheads or hidden gems.

Karavostasis & Agali

Karavostasis, the port, is the gateway to the island. If you're staying nearby:

- Walk to Vardia Beach within 5 minutes
- Catch boat taxis to Katergo or Livadaki

Agali is a beach hamlet with a few hotels and tavernas. From here:

- Hike to Fira and Galifos beaches
- Catch small boats to even more remote spots

Useful Travel Apps

- **Google Maps**: Good for village navigation and car routes.

- **Maps.me**: Better for offline hiking trails, download the island in advance.

- **Ferryhopper**: Essential for checking ferry schedules and updates.

- **Rome2Rio**: Great for planning airport-to-port routes.

The Journey Is Part of the Story

Traveling to Folegandros is an initiation. It's not the place you arrive at by accident, it's a destination you choose. And the effort makes it sweeter. Whether you approach by ferry at dawn with the sea mist curling around the cliffs, or sail across on a golden afternoon from Milos or Santorini, the moment you step onto the island, something shifts. The pace slows. The senses awaken.

And once you're here, getting around is effortless in all the right ways. With each scooter ride, hillside walk, or bus ride through wind-carved villages, you're not just exploring the island, you're sinking into its rhythm. Let that rhythm guide you, and the island will reveal itself slowly, like a story worth savoring.

Chapter 4: Where to Stay in Folegandros

I've always said that where you rest your head can shape your entire experience of a place, and Folegandros, with its wild beauty and serene spirit, is no exception. Whether you seek the comfort of a boutique hideaway, the charm of a family-run guesthouse, or the indulgence of a cliffside villa where the Aegean seems to spill into your bedroom, this island delivers in style. In Folegandros, your accommodation isn't just a place to sleep, it becomes a quiet companion to your journey, steeped in Cycladic character and warmed by genuine hospitality.

This chapter is your compass to the best places to stay on the island, complete with my insights and favorite recommendations. Let's begin by orienting ourselves among the island's main villages before diving into the stays that suit every traveler, from the budget-conscious to the luxury-seeker.

4.1 Overview of Island Villages & Best Areas to Stay

Folegandros may be small, but its three main settlements, Karavostasis, Chora, and Ano Meria, offer distinct atmospheres and experiences.

Chora: The Heart of the Island

Perched high on the cliffs, Chora is the island's soul: a labyrinth of whitewashed alleyways, stone-paved squares, and cascading bougainvillaea. Staying here means waking up to bell chimes echoing from the Panagia church and stepping out into a car-free maze of cafés, shops, and tavernas.

- Best for: Couples, solo travelers, and those seeking a central location with vibrant charm.
- Pros: Easy access to nightlife, dining, and public transport.
- Cons: Limited parking, and some accommodation is a short walk from drop-off points.

Karavostasis: The Quiet Port

Where the ferries dock and the sea laps gently at pebbled shores, Karavostasis offers a more tranquil experience. Accommodations here are a stone's throw from the water, perfect for early morning swims or watching boats drift by at sunset.

- Best for: Beach lovers, families, and early risers.
- Pros: Proximity to the port, beaches, and boat tours.
- Cons: Quieter in the evenings; fewer dining options compared to Chora.

Ano Meria: Rustic and Remote

This traditional farming village stretches along a ridge with sweeping views and agricultural authenticity. Life moves slower here, and the accommodations reflect that: simple, heartfelt, and close to the land.

- Best for: Nature lovers, hikers, and those wanting to unplug.
- Pros: Authentic village charm, hiking trail access.
- Cons: Limited transport; restaurants and shops can be sparse.

4.2 Budget-Friendly Stays: Hostels, Studios & Guesthouses

For the traveler who values experience over opulence, Folegandros offers several delightful and affordable options that don't skimp on character.

Family-Run Studios

Throughout Chora and Karavostasis, you'll find whitewashed buildings with blue shutters hiding cozy studios with kitchenettes and terraces. Many are run by local families who treat guests like kin, offering raki on arrival and tips whispered with pride.

- **Recommended:** Sofia Rooms in Chora – basic but central, with breezy balconies and genuine warmth.

- Prices: Starting at €50–70 per night in shoulder season; book early in summer.

Budget Tips

- Travel in May or September for lower rates and milder weather.
- Many studios offer discounts for stays longer than three nights.
- Bring cash, some smaller guesthouses don't accept credit cards.

4.3 Mid-Range & Boutique Hotels

If you're looking for comfort with a touch of elegance, Folegandros' mid-range hotels are designed with both style and soul. These aren't cookie-cutter accommodations, they're handcrafted spaces that blend Cycladic architecture with thoughtful amenities.

Stylish Simplicity

In Chora, boutique hotels balance minimalist design with stunning surroundings. Whitewashed walls, stone accents, and driftwood décor echo the natural beauty outside. Many offer sweeping sea views and saltwater pools nestled in flowering courtyards.

- **Recommended:** Anemomilos Boutique Hotel – Perched above Chora, this hotel offers jaw-dropping views, immaculate rooms, and a breakfast of dreams (think fresh fruit, local honey, and just-baked bread).

- **Also try:** Blue Sand Boutique Hotel near Agali Beach – where waves provide your morning alarm clock.

Tips for Mid-Range Travelers

- Ask about **shuttle services** from the port; some hotels include this at no charge.

- Many properties provide local guides or hiking maps; take advantage.

- Expect prices between €90 and € 150 per night, depending on season and amenities.

4.4 Luxury Villas, Spa Hotels & Cliffside Resorts

Folegandros may be low-key, but it knows how to do luxury, with discretion and grace. There are no sprawling five-star resorts, but instead, intimate retreats where every detail feels curated for peace and pleasure.

Cliffside Elegance

High above the Aegean, near Chora's edge, sit a handful of villas and boutique hotels that rival anything found in Santorini, minus the crowds.

- **Recommended:** Aria Suites – Private plunge pools, Cycladic-meets-modern décor, and sunset views that turn the sky to gold.
- **Luxury Tip:** Request a room facing west to catch the full magic of the setting sun.

Wellness Escapes

A few high-end accommodations offer spa treatments, yoga classes, and personal chefs, perfect for a holistic recharge.

- Prices typically start at €200 per night, rising to €500+ in high season.
- Many include bespoke experiences like wine tastings, guided hikes, and sailing charters.

4.5 Unique & Sustainable Stays (Eco-Lodges, Airbnb Gems)

For travelers seeking something different, something that tells a story, Folegandros has a small but growing number of eco-conscious lodgings and creative stays that marry comfort with sustainability.

Eco-Friendly Hideaways

Built with local stone and powered by the sun, these off-grid villas offer privacy, silence, and a chance to reconnect with nature.

- **Recommended:** Under the Sun Cycladic Village – Off-grid suites carved into the landscape with panoramic views and zero environmental compromise.

- Composting, rainwater collection, and passive cooling are standard, without sacrificing style.

Airbnb Favorites

Look for restored shepherd's huts and hidden homes in Ano Meria, where stone walls keep rooms cool and outdoor patios overlook olive groves.

- Many hosts are happy to share their garden bounty, expect tomatoes, figs, and fresh herbs.

- Tip: Filter listings by Superhost status and check for amenities like Wi-Fi (which can be patchy in remote areas).

Let Your Stay Become the Story

No matter where you choose to stay in Folegandros, perched on a cliff, tucked into a farming village, or steps from the sea, your accommodation will become part of your story. These aren't just places to sleep. They're extensions of the island's slow rhythm, its wind-swept landscapes, and its deeply rooted hospitality.

My advice? Don't just pick a place, pick a mood. Wake with the roosters in Ano Meria, or sip wine by a candlelit pool in Chora. Let the stillness of your surroundings seep into your bones. Because in Folegandros, the real luxury isn't just the view, it's how you feel when you wake up to it.

Chapter 5: Top Attractions & Must-Sees - The Essential Folegandros Experience

There's something undeniably captivating about Folegandros. It's not an island that clamors for attention; it whispers its secrets gently, inviting you to slow down and savor the details. Each bend in the trail, each turn in the village alleyways, leads to something quietly breathtaking. In this chapter, I'll take you through the must-see sights and experiences of the island, places that are not only beautiful but essential to understanding the soul of Folegandros.

5.1 Chora: The Cliffside Capital

Winding up from the port into the sky, Chora greets you like a dream made of whitewashed stone and cobalt blue shutters. Nestled atop a cliff with dizzying views of the Aegean Sea, it's one of the most enchanting villages I've ever wandered through, and that's saying something.

Chora is a place to get lost, intentionally. The streets are narrow and car-free, lined with tiny churches, family-owned tavernas, and squares that feel frozen in time. Life here is measured in coffee cups and sunset glows.

What not to miss in Chora:

- **Piazza-hopping:** The village has several interconnected squares, each with its own ambiance. Pounta Square is perfect for a mid-morning coffee, while Dounavi Square comes alive with laughter and clinking glasses at night.

- **Traditional bakeries:** Try To Zimaraki for fresh spinach pies or sesame koulouri. Follow your nose.

- **Local boutiques:** Handwoven textiles, ceramics, and jewelry by local artisans make for meaningful souvenirs.

Traveler Tips:

- Evenings in Chora can get breezy. Bring a light jacket, even in summer.

- The best photo ops are just before sunset, wander the cliff path behind the village for golden light and sweeping views.

5.2 Panagia Church & the Scenic Hike

Of all the sights in Folegandros, the Church of Panagia holds a special place in my heart. Not only for its historical and religious significance but for the journey it requires, a winding, zigzagging footpath that feels both meditative and exhilarating.

The church sits perched above Chora, almost floating against the sky. Its gleaming white exterior, set against the stark hillside and endless sea, is the postcard view of Folegandros. But this is more than just a beautiful photograph.

The experience:

- The walk begins in Chora, and though it's short (about 15–20 minutes), the climb is steady. Time it right and go during golden hour for a scene that glows with color.

- Along the way, you'll pass stone terraces, grazing goats, and wild herbs that perfume the air.

- Once at the top, take a moment. The panoramic views span the sea, the cliffs, and the vast sky. It's a place that invites silence and awe.

Cultural Insight: The church is dedicated to the Virgin Mary and is the spiritual heart of the island. Locals walk this same path barefoot during religious festivals, especially on March 25th and August 15th.

Travel Tip: Bring water and wear shoes with a grip. While the path is well-maintained, the stones can be slippery.

5.3 Kastro Village & Historical Walks

Tucked within Chora's boundaries lies Kastro, the medieval heart of the island. This ancient settlement dates back to the 13th century when the Venetians built it as a fortress village to protect locals from pirate raids. Today, it remains remarkably preserved, a quiet, lived-in museum of everyday history.

Why visit Kastro:

- **Architecture:** The buildings here are among the oldest on the island. Homes are built into the walls of the fortress, complete with wooden balconies and tiny doors that open directly onto the stone pathways.

- **History underfoot:** Look down as you walk. Many stones are original, worn smooth by centuries of feet. Some doorways still bear family crests or initials carved into marble.

- **Churches and corners:** Tiny chapels appear around bends, often unlocked and candle-lit. Step inside for a moment of stillness.

Hidden Gem: Seek out the house where Greek writer Georgios Drosinis once stayed; there's no sign, but locals will happily point you there if you ask.

Travel Tip: Visit early in the morning or late afternoon to avoid the heat and to enjoy the light slanting through the ancient alleyways.

5.4 Agali Beach & the Coastal Trails

If Chora is the cultural soul of Folegandros, then Agali Beach is its playful, sun-drenched heart. Set in a crescent-shaped bay framed by cliffs, Agali is one of the island's most beloved beaches, and for good reason.

Why Agali is special:

- **Swimmable waters:** The clear, calm sea is ideal for swimming. The water deepens gently, making it suitable for families.

- **Tavernas by the shore:** Imagine emerging from the water and walking barefoot into a taverna for grilled octopus and a glass of local white wine. That's the Agali rhythm.

- **Hiking access:** From Agali, coastal trails lead to Galifos and Agios Nikolaos, two beaches that feel untouched and wild. They're only accessible by foot or boat, which adds to the allure.

My advice:

- Pack good walking sandals and set out in the morning before the sun is too high.

- Bring water and shade if hiking; there's little cover on the trails.

- At Agios Nikolaos, eat at the seaside taverna (it has no name) and order the saganaki with honey, it's unforgettable.

Best season to go: Late May and early September are ideal, warm seas, fewer crowds, and soft light that lingers well into the evening.

5.5 Sunset Viewpoints & Iconic Landscapes

Sunsets in Folegandros aren't just beautiful, they're sacred. The island's western exposure offers some of the most spellbinding vistas in the Cyclades, and each evening feels like a ceremony of color and silence.

Top Sunset Spots:

- **Panagia Church terrace:** This is the crown jewel of Folegandros sunsets. From here, the sun dips directly into the Aegean, often setting behind scattered islets in a blaze of pink and fire-orange.

- **Chora's cliffside promenade:** Follow the stone path that skirts the village edge. It's less crowded than the church and ideal for photographers.

- **Agios Savvas viewpoint:** A lesser-known lookout near Ano Meria. Come here with a picnic and a thermos of wine, it's often just you and the wind.

Photography Tip: Use a neutral density filter if shooting with a DSLR to capture the full range of color without washing out the highlights.

Cultural Moment: On summer evenings, locals often gather in the squares after sunset. It's the perfect time to join them for a rakomelo (raki infused with honey and spices) and reflect on the day.

Let the Island Reveal Itself

Folegandros doesn't beg for your attention. It earns it through quiet beauty, timeless stories, and moments that feel entirely your own. The attractions here aren't about long lines or bucket lists, they're about connection. To the land. To the light. To the people who live with gentle pride and welcome strangers like old friends.

So wander slowly. Let yourself be drawn not only to the places described here but also to those that surprise you. The magic of Folegandros is often in the details, an arched doorway, a taverna tucked beneath vines, or a path that ends with the sea.

Chapter 6: Hidden Gems & Local Secrets - Where Folegandros Truly Reveals Its Soul

Every island has its showstoppers, those shimmering beaches and ancient churches that fill postcards and photo albums. But the essence of Folegandros lies in the places that don't make the headlines. The unmarked trails, the nameless tavernas, the conversations had under pergolas while the scent of thyme drifts through the air. These are the memories that linger.

In this chapter, I'll take you beyond the guidebook pages and into the quiet heart of the island, its hidden beaches, forgotten paths, timeless traditions, and secret sunset spots. These aren't just places, they're invitations to live like a local and see the island through different eyes.

6.1 Remote Beaches: Livadaki, Vardia & Agios Nikolaos

Let's begin with the shores, those wild, whispering places where the sea laps the rocks and time slows to the rhythm of the waves.

While Agali Beach offers easy access and tavernas, the more remote stretches of Folegandros require effort, and are all the more rewarding for it.

Livadaki Beach: The Secluded Sanctuary

Tucked away on the island's northern edge, Livadaki is one of the most beautiful and elusive beaches in the Cyclades. It's not easy to get to: you'll need to hike for nearly an hour from Ano Meria or take a boat from the port in Karavostasis. But once you arrive, it feels like you've stumbled into a secret world.

- **Why visit:** Crystal-clear turquoise water, dramatic cliffs, and a sense of total isolation. There's no infrastructure, just raw beauty.

- **Pro Tip:** Bring water, shade, and snacks. There's no taverna, no music, no amenities. Just you, the rocks, and the sea.

Vardia Beach: The Port's Hidden Cove

Just steps from the arrival point in Karavostasis lies Vardia, a small beach many travelers overlook. Sheltered by cliffs and blessed with golden sand, it's perfect for a quick dip or a quiet read while you wait for a ferry.

- **Best time:** Early morning or sunset, when the boats are gone and the water turns glassy.

- **Local secret:** Walk to the far end of the beach and you'll find a rocky ledge ideal for snorkeling and sunbathing in solitude.

Agios Nikolaos Beach: The Laid-Back Escape

Reachable by boat from Agali or a moderate hike, Agios Nikolaos is the kind of place where lunch turns into a nap and time stretches like a lazy cat in the sun. Olive trees line the shore, and the beach itself is a mix of pebbles and fine sand.

- **Dining tip:** There's a rustic taverna here, where I've had some of the best grilled sardines of my life, simple, smoky, perfect.

- **What to bring:** Reef-safe sunscreen and patience. The peace here is worth the trek.

6.2 Untouched Villages & Lesser-Known Paths

Most visitors stay close to Chora or the beaches, but venture just a little further, and you'll uncover villages and trails that seem suspended in time.

Ano Meria: A Village in a Time Capsule

Located on the northern plateau, Ano Meria is more than just a farming village, it's the heartland of Folegandros' traditions. Life here unfolds slowly, in harmony with the land.

- **Highlights:** Visit the Folklore Museum, housed in a traditional farmhouse, to glimpse how islanders lived in centuries past. Stone mills, donkey stables, and bread ovens reveal a world of self-sufficiency.

- **Cultural etiquette:** Greet locals with a warm "Kalimera" and don't be surprised if they offer you a fig or a story.

Hiking the Forgotten Paths

Folegandros is laced with a network of ancient footpaths, some barely marked but still navigable. One of my favorite routes is the trail from Ano Meria to Livadaki, where every step offers views of the wind-shaped landscape and the cerulean sea.

- **Tips for walkers:**
    - Carry plenty of water and wear proper hiking shoes.
    - Spring (April–June) offers blooming wildflowers and cooler temperatures.
    - Download a hiking app or get a local map; many trails aren't well marked.

Don't Miss: The Katergo trail near the port leads to another dramatic beach, best done early in the day before the sun becomes too intense.

6.3 Authentic Local Experiences: Ceramics, Honey, and Raki

To truly connect with a place, you need to taste it, touch it, and understand the hands that shape it. Folegandros might be small, but its artisanal traditions are rich and alive.

Ceramic Workshops

In a quiet courtyard in Chora, I met Maria, a third-generation potter who shapes the island's clay into graceful, simple forms. Her studio doubles as a gallery, where each piece tells a story of function and form.

- **What to buy:** Water jugs, oil lamps, and hand-painted tiles inspired by Cycladic motifs.

- **Experience:** Some workshops offer short demos, just ask. Watching a pot take shape beneath practiced hands is mesmerizing.

Honey & Herbal Remedies

Bees thrive in the thyme- and oregano-rich hills of Folegandros, producing fragrant, amber-hued honey. In Ano Meria, I stumbled upon a family-run shop selling small jars labeled by harvest date and location.

- **Try:** Wild thyme honey on fresh bread or stirred into Greek yogurt.

- **Look out for:** Locally made salves and teas using diktamo, sage, and wild mint.

The Spirit of Raki

Raki is more than a drink here, it's a social ritual. Distilled from grape pomace after the wine harvest, it's strong, clear, and usually shared with laughter.

- **Where to try:** Tavernas often offer it as a post-meal treat. In autumn, ask locals about Kazania, the distillation celebrations. You may just get invited.

- **Travel tip:** Sip slowly. It sneaks up on you.

6.4 Under-the-Radar Dining & Sunset Spots

Folegandros may not have flashy beach clubs or Michelin stars, but what it does have is soul. The best meals are often the simplest, and the best views are often shared with just a few goats and the wind.

Secret Dining Finds

- To Aspropotamos (Ano Meria): No menu, just what's fresh. On my visit, it was revithada (baked chickpeas) and grilled eggplant, unforgettable.

- Eva's Garden (Chora): Slightly hidden, surrounded by bougainvillea, it serves modern twists on local dishes like fava with caramelized onions and lemon zest.

- Sinantisi (Karavostasis): A seaside gem where the octopus is dried in the sun before hitting the grill.

Sunset Havens

- **Pounta Square** in Chora: Grab a drink from a nearby bar and settle on a stone bench with the locals.

- **Agios Savvas Hill**: A short hike from Ano Meria leads to a rugged bluff overlooking the west. Few tourists ever come here, and the sunset feels like it was painted just for you.

- **Cliffside behind Panagia Church**: Everyone goes to the church, but walk five minutes further to find your own private perch.

Following the Whispers

The hidden side of Folegandros doesn't shout, it whispers. And if you listen carefully, you'll find yourself invited into a slower, deeper rhythm of life. These secret corners and local treasures are the ones that stay with you long after you leave, the soft crunch of a goat path underfoot, the warm burn of raki at dusk, the kindness in a stranger's eyes

Chapter 7: Flavors of Folegandros – Food & Drink

There's a rhythm to life on Folegandros that's inextricably tied to food, slower, richer, and deeply rooted in the island's heritage. Here, every meal tells a story: of the farmer tending his terraced fields under the Cycladic sun, the fisherman hauling in his morning catch, the grandmother rolling fresh pasta with weathered hands. Food is not just nourishment, it's memory, tradition, and celebration.

This chapter is your invitation to savor the tastes of Folegandros as I have: through long lunches in flower-draped courtyards, seaside dinners where waves are the soundtrack, and warm conversations over shared plates and carafes of local wine. The island may be small, but its culinary soul is immense.

7.1 Must-Try Local Dishes

From Hand-Rolled Matsata to the Creaminess of Souroto

Let's begin with the foundations, the dishes that define the island's unique gastronomy. You won't find flashy fusion menus here. Instead, Folegandros champions simple, honest ingredients elevated by care and time.

Matsata: The Heart of the Table

If Folegandros had a national dish, it would be matsata. Handmade egg pasta, thicker and softer than Italian tagliatelle, is simmered in a rich, slow-cooked tomato sauce. Traditionally, it's served with goat or rooster, often prepared hours ahead in a deep, fragrant stew.

- **Pro tip:** Order it in the early afternoon. It's a dish best enjoyed after a long morning walk and with a glass of local red.

- **Cultural note:** Every family has its own version. If you're lucky, you may get invited to try a home-cooked one in Ano Meria.

Souroto Cheese: The Unsung Hero

Forget feta, **souroto** is Folegandros' signature soft cheese. Mild, slightly tangy, and wonderfully spreadable, it's used generously in salads, pies, and on fresh bread drizzled with thyme honey.

- **Where to find it:** Order the local salad in most tavernas. It's usually topped with a hefty dollop of souroto instead of crumbled feta.

Other Essentials to Try:

- **Kalasouna:** A savory pie filled with onions and souroto, encased in a golden, flaky crust.

- **Revithada:** Oven-baked chickpeas with onion, olive oil, and a hint of lemon. A dish of deep comfort, often made in clay pots.

- **Psaropita:** Fish pie, made from salted or fresh fish, seasoned with herbs, and wrapped in homemade dough.

- **Capers:** Often foraged wild, they are pickled and sprinkled over salads or pasta.

7.2 Top Taverns, Family-Run Eateries & Beachside Grills

Where the Island's Heart is Best Tasted

Dining in Folegandros is rarely formal, but it's always heartfelt. The tavernas here are extensions of the homes that run them, and a meal is often accompanied by stories, smiles, and maybe even a bit of local gossip.

O Kritikos (Chora):
This tiny taverna tucked into a backstreet is a local institution. The owners greet guests like family, and the matsata here is among the island's best. Try their slow-braised rabbit and grilled zucchini flowers.

To Aspropotamos (Ano Meria):

In a quiet corner of the farming village lies this taverna that serves dishes straight from the fields. They don't print menus, just sit down, ask what's cooking, and be prepared for a rustic, unforgettable meal.

Papalagi Seafood (Karavostasis):

Overlooking the port, this beachside grill serves freshly caught fish and seafood risotto with sea views that rival the food. Ideal for sunset dining.

Piatsa (Chora):

Set in a vibrant square, Piatsa is casual and inviting. Their souroto and caper salad, followed by grilled lamb chops, is the stuff of island dreams.

Budget tip: Most tavernas serve ample portions meant for sharing. Order a few plates for the table instead of individual mains, it's both economical and culturally appropriate.

7.3 Wine Bars, Cafés & Cocktails with a View

Sip, Savor, and Watch the World Go By

After a day exploring rugged trails or swimming in secret coves, there's no better reward than a well-earned drink. Whether you prefer a glass of wine under the stars or a cappuccino with the scent of jasmine in the air, Folegandros delivers.

Wine Bars & Ouzeries

- **Rakentia Wine Bar (Chora):** Small, stylish, and boasting an impressive selection of Greek wines, this spot is perfect for an aperitif. Try a glass of Assyrtiko paired with local olives and cheese.

- **Hondros Loukas (Ano Meria):** More of a rustic ouzeri than a bar, this place is known for its homemade raki and convivial atmosphere. A great place to practice your Greek and hear local tales.

Cafés with Character

- **Pounta Café (Chora):** Perched on a cliffside, this is one of my favorite morning stops. The coffee is strong, the orange juice fresh-squeezed, and the view over the Aegean endless.

- **Mimi's Kafeneio (Ano Meria):** A throwback to older times, no frills, just excellent Greek coffee, sweet spoon preserves, and friendly chatter.

Cocktails with a View

- **Bee Bar (Chora):** Trendy yet relaxed, Bee Bar crafts cocktails with Greek spirits and fresh herbs. Try the Folegandros Mule made with mastiha and ginger.

- **Astarti Bar (Chora):** Ideal for late-night lounging, with ambient music and seats facing the horizon. The mojitos are popular, but I prefer their herbal negroni.

Luxury tip: Many boutique hotels also have cocktail terraces open to non-guests, especially around sunset.

7.4 Food Markets & Culinary Tours

Where the Journey of Taste Begins

Though Folegandros doesn't have massive food markets like Athens or Thessaloniki, the island makes up for it with small, meaningful experiences that connect you directly to the source.

Local Grocers & Bakeries

- **Chora's Morning Market:** Along the stone-paved streets of Chora, you'll find small shops selling local honey, capers, olive oil, and preserved fruits. Look for unlabeled jars, these are often homemade and exceptional.

- **To Paradosiako (Bakery in Chora):** An old-style bakery where you can watch bread being pulled from a wood-fired oven at dawn. Try the anise rusks or cheese-stuffed pastries.

Culinary Tours & Experiences

- **Cooking with Maria (Ano Meria):** A half-day cooking class run in a traditional home. You'll learn to make matsata and kalasouna from scratch, followed by a leisurely meal on a shaded terrace. It's not a polished, commercial affair; it's authentic, and that's what makes it special.

- **Herbal Foraging Walks:** In spring, local guides sometimes lead foraging walks to identify and collect wild herbs like oregano, sage, and dittany. These end with herbal tea tastings and stories of island healing traditions.

Seasonal note: Visit in late summer or autumn for fig season and wine harvest festivities. Some villages still celebrate kazania, raki distillation parties filled with music and food.

Savoring the Soul of the Island

Folegandros doesn't shout its culinary story, it sings it, gently and with conviction. Each meal here is a slow unfolding of the island's past and present: in the taverna that still cooks with grandma's recipes, in the cheese shaped by hand in a mountain village, in the clink of glasses under the Milky Way.

Come hungry, but more importantly, come curious. Because on Folegandros, food is not just what's served, it's how you're welcomed, remembered, and woven into the island's story.

Chapter 8: Shopping & Island Finds – Treasures of Folegandros

Shopping on Folegandros is not about high-street brands or glitzy malls. It's about moments, uncovering a handwoven textile in a sunlit atelier, chatting with a silversmith as they etch Cycladic spirals into a bracelet, or sipping rakomelo while you wait for a jar of capers to be wrapped in brown paper and string. Every purchase here is a story, an encounter, and a keepsake that carries the scent of the Aegean and the rhythm of the island's slow, intentional way of life.

As a seasoned traveler with a deep love for the Cyclades, I can say with certainty: this is one of the few places where shopping feels soulful. Whether you're after timeless handmade pieces, affordable keepsakes, or something luxurious and bespoke, Folegandros rewards those who wander off the main path, and ask the right questions.

8.1 Souvenir Ideas & Where to Buy Them

From Tasteful Tokens to Meaningful Mementos

One of the joys of travel is taking a piece of the journey home, not just something to display on a shelf, but something that rekindles a memory every time you touch, taste, or smell it. Folegandros offers just that, through a mix of edible delights, artisanal crafts, and thoughtful souvenirs.

Top Souvenir Picks:

- **Local Honey & Thyme:** Thick, golden honey made from wild thyme that blankets the hillsides. Available in small jars perfect for travel. I always bring back at least two, one for me, one as a gift.

- **Capers in Brine or Salt:** Folegandros is known for its wild capers. Ask for ones preserved by local families; they have a more intense flavor and a story to tell.

- **Herbal Sachets & Oils:** Dried bundles of oregano, sage, and lavender, ideal for seasoning or freshening drawers.

- **Ceramic Plates with Cycladic Motifs:** Hand-painted and often uniquely signed by the artist. Great for decorative use or as serving dishes.

- **Mini Bottles of Rakomelo or Local Wine:** Look for home-distilled varieties sold in repurposed glass bottles, rustic, yes, but authentic.

Where to Buy:

- **Souvenir Stalls in Chora:** Scattered throughout the narrow alleys, you'll find small shops that specialize in local goods. I recommend stopping by Pantopoleion To Steki, a charming store with regional products and friendly service.

- **Port Shops in Karavostasis:** Ideal for last-minute buys before catching your ferry, but don't expect much variety or artisan flair.

Travel Tip: Always ask if a product is made on the island. Some shops import mass-produced "Greek" goods from the mainland. Trust your instincts, and your nose, especially when it comes to herbs and honey.

8.2 Handmade Crafts, Jewelry & Local Art

The Artisan Spirit of Folegandros

There's something magical about meeting the person who made your souvenir. On Folegandros, creativity is quiet but deeply rooted. You won't find sprawling artisan markets, but if you look closely and follow the scent of beeswax or the rhythmic hammering of metal, you'll discover hidden studios and workshops where tradition lives on in every stitch and swirl.

Jewelry & Metalwork:

Wandering through Chora, I discovered Artifex Workshop, a small boutique where a soft-spoken artist creates jewelry inspired by ancient Cycladic symbols. Her work, spirals, waves, and olive branches, is forged in silver and copper, each piece with a gentle imperfection that makes it feel alive.

Textiles & Weaving:

In Ano Meria, there's a family home where a grandmother still weaves on a wooden loom. Ask around (especially at local tavernas) and you might get directions. She makes traditional phoustani-style scarves and table runners dyed with herbs and minerals. It's not a business, it's a tradition she's keeping alive.

Painting & Ceramics:

Local artist Eleni Papadaki paints minimalist island landscapes with natural pigments. Her tiny studio doubles as a gallery, and her seascapes capture the island's light in a way a camera never could. If ceramics are more your style, check out Folegandros Pottery near the entrance to Chora, earthy, functional pieces perfect for modern kitchens.

Pro Tip:

Artisans often close their studios midday or during the off-season. Call ahead or drop by in the late afternoon when the breeze cools and shopkeepers are more relaxed.

8.3 Where to Shop on a Budget

Affordable Finds with Character

Not every traveler has the room (in their suitcase or their budget) for original art or designer jewelry. Fortunately, Folegandros offers plenty of charming, budget-friendly options that won't feel like tourist tat.

Budget Shopping Spots:

- **General Stores in Chora:** Shops like Perivoli tou Ouranou and Katerina's Corner sell affordable soaps, wooden kitchen tools, postcards, and small ceramics. You can also find playful magnets, bookmarks with island quotes, and hand-painted stones.

- **Local Markets & Bakeries:** Visit a traditional bakery for anise rusks or koulourakia (Greek butter cookies) that make delicious gifts. A few euros buy you a bundle wrapped in wax paper.

- **Sunday Craft Market (Seasonal):** During high season, a small Sunday market sometimes pops up near Chora's main square. Young artisans and seasonal workers sell handmade bracelets, photo prints, and upcycled jewelry.

Best Budget Picks:

- Hand-tied herb bundles: €2–€3

- Mini olive oil or honey jars: €4–€5

- Beaded bracelets or shell necklaces: €6–€10

- Local cookies or sweets: under €5

Money-Saving Tip: Buy in bundles. Some shops offer discounts if you purchase multiple items, especially food products or handmade soaps.

8.4 High-End Boutiques & Artisan Studios

When Only the Best Will Do

If you're looking to splurge or take home something exquisite, Folegandros has a handful of high-end spots worth visiting. They're discreet, no flashy storefronts or neon signs, but once inside, you'll discover craftsmanship that rivals galleries in Athens or Santorini.

Best Boutiques for Upscale Shopping:

- **Seladi (Chora):** A sleek, minimalist space that blends fashion, ceramics, and design objects. Their linen clothing line, inspired by Cycladic architecture, is both wearable and timeless. Prices are steep, but quality is unmatched.

- **The Silk Thread (Chora):** Specializes in hand-dyed scarves and shawls made from Greek silk. The owner travels to mainland workshops to source her materials, then designs and dyes them on the island.

- **Kallisti Goldsmiths (Chora):** Elegant, bespoke jewelry with a story. Ask for their signature Aegean Wave pendant, it's a sculptural homage to the sea that surrounds the island.

Insider Tip:

Many of these high-end shops offer shipping options, which is ideal if you're worried about carrying fragile or high-value items on your return journey.

More Than Just a Purchase

To shop in Folegandros is to slow down and connect to the land, to the people, and the moment. It's browsing through sun-dappled shops while cicadas sing in the background, or sipping a tiny glass of liqueur offered by the shopkeeper as you contemplate a hand-painted bowl. Whether you leave with a silk scarf or a simple sprig of dried oregano, the value lies in the memory that comes with it.

So, take your time. Wander without purpose. Ask questions. And let the island guide you to the objects that will become your most treasured souvenirs.

Chapter 9: Outdoor Adventures – Embracing Folegandros' Wild Beauty

If there's one thing I've learned from countless visits to the Cyclades, it's that the real magic of islands like Folegandros lies in their rugged, untamed outdoor landscapes. The island's cliffs, crystal-clear waters, and sparse yet lush greenery invite you to step outside the confines of traditional sightseeing and immerse yourself fully in nature's splendor. From dawn hikes that reveal panoramic sea views to secret coves perfect for a refreshing swim, Folegandros offers outdoor adventures that linger in your memory long after you leave.

Let me take you on a journey through my favorite ways to explore Folegandros outdoors, whether on foot, by sea, or through mindful connection with the island's serene rhythms. This chapter will equip you with practical insights, insider tips, and evocative descriptions that will make you eager to lace up your hiking boots or dive headfirst into the Aegean's crystalline embrace.

9.1 Hiking Routes with Stunning Sea Views

Trails that Reveal the Island's Soul

Folegandros is a hiker's paradise, albeit one with a distinct Cycladic character, dry stone paths winding along cliffs, wild herbs scenting the breeze, and sweeping views that seem to stretch forever across the deep blue. The island's compact size means you can explore diverse trails without long transfers, and every route comes with its own reward: an ancient chapel, a hidden beach, or a panoramic vista that makes you pause and breathe deeply.

My Top Hiking Routes:

- **Chora to Ano Meria:** This classic route takes you from the island's main village up to its traditional heartland. As you climb, the Aegean unfolds below like a vast, shimmering carpet. The highlight is the whitewashed Church of Panagia, perched on a hill, where the silence feels sacred. Pack plenty of water and start early to avoid the midday heat.

- **Katergo Bay Trail:** One of my personal favorites, this moderate trail descends from Chora down to Katergo beach, a stunning pebble cove framed by dramatic cliffs. The turquoise water here is among the clearest on the island, perfect for a rewarding swim after your hike. The trail is rocky but manageable, so wear sturdy shoes.

- **Ano Meria to Agali Beach:** For those who want a longer, less traveled path, this route leads from the pastoral northern village through wild landscapes to Agali, a tranquil bay dotted with traditional tavernas. Along the way, you'll see remnants of ancient terraces and, if lucky, wild goats grazing peacefully.

Hiking Tips:

- Start early in the morning or late afternoon to avoid the sun's peak.
- Bring a hat, sunscreen, and a reusable water bottle (the island's water is excellent and potable).
- Wear comfortable hiking shoes; many paths are uneven and rocky.
- Respect local customs by not picking wild plants and staying on marked trails.
- Consider hiring a local guide for deeper cultural insights and hidden spots.

9.2 Snorkeling & Swimming in Hidden Coves

The Underwater World Beckons

The Aegean Sea around Folegandros is a treasure trove of marine life and clear waters, ideal for snorkeling and swimming. What I love most about this island is that its secluded coves remain unspoiled and quiet, perfect for escaping the crowds and slipping into nature's quiet embrace.

Secret Swim Spots to Discover:

- **Livadaki Cove:** Just a short walk from the main harbor, Livadaki offers crystal-clear waters and a rocky seabed teeming with colorful fish and sea urchins. The beach itself is small and pebble-strewn, so bring water shoes.

- **Agios Nikolaos Bay:** Tucked away on the southwestern coast, this bay's calm waters make it a favorite for snorkeling beginners. Beneath the surface, you'll find interesting rock formations and occasional octopus sightings.

- **Katergo Beach:** After your hike down here, take the chance to snorkel the shallow edges. The underwater visibility is excellent, and the fish are curious but not skittish.

Swimming and Snorkeling Essentials:

- Bring your own snorkel gear, or rent from shops in Chora.

- Early morning swims offer the calmest water and the best light for underwater viewing.

- Always check local weather and sea conditions; the Meltemi wind can make some spots rough.

- Respect the marine environment, avoid touching corals or disturbing wildlife.

9.3 Boat Tours, Island Hopping & Sea Caves

Exploring Folegandros from the Water

If there's a secret I cherish about Folegandros, it's that the island reveals a completely different personality from the sea. Jagged cliffs give way to mysterious caves, small islands pepper the horizon, and secluded beaches are only accessible by boat. Whether you charter a private vessel or join a group tour, setting out on the water is an adventure you won't want to miss.

Types of Boat Tours:

- **Half-Day Excursions:** These tours often include stops at sea caves like the famous Cyclops Cave, where myth and geology intertwine. The guides usually provide snorkeling gear, drinks, and a simple Greek lunch on board.

- **Island Hopping:** Folegandros is perfectly positioned for day trips to nearby islands like Sikinos and Ios. Each has its own vibe; Sikinos is tranquil and rural, while Ios is lively with beautiful beaches.

- **Private Boat Rentals:** For a more intimate experience, renting a small boat or sailing yacht lets you explore hidden coves at your own pace. I recommend hiring a skipper if you're not confident navigating the rocky coastline.

Boat Tour Tips:

- Book tours in advance during high season, but some last-minute options are often available.

- Bring sun protection, swimwear, and a waterproof camera.

- Respect local marine regulations and never anchor in protected zones.

- Ask your captain about less-visited coves or best snorkeling spots; locals often have secret knowledge.

9.4 Yoga, Wellness & Nature Immersion

Finding Balance Amidst Untamed Beauty

For travelers craving more than physical adventure, Folegandros offers spaces and moments of wellness, mindfulness, and holistic connection. The island's slow pace and natural beauty create the perfect backdrop for yoga, meditation, and simply being present.

Wellness Experiences I Recommend:

- **Morning Yoga at Chora:** Several boutique guesthouses and wellness centers offer open-air classes with breathtaking views of the caldera and sea. Starting your day with a gentle flow here feels like aligning your energy with the island itself.

- **Guided Nature Walks:** Some local guides combine hiking with mindfulness exercises, encouraging you to tune into the island's sounds, the wind in the trees, birdsong, the distant splash of waves.

- **Holistic Spa Treatments:** A few hidden gems in Folegandros offer massages and traditional Greek therapies using olive oil, mountain herbs, and honey. These are perfect for unwinding after a day of outdoor exploration.

- **Sunset Meditation on the Cliffs:** One evening, I found myself seated at the edge of the island's western cliffs, watching the sun sink slowly into the sea. Guided or solo, such moments are deeply restorative.

Wellness Travel Tips:

- Pack lightweight, breathable clothing suitable for yoga or meditation outdoors.

- Bring a travel mat if you plan to do yoga independently.

- Check with your accommodation for wellness offerings or local contacts.

- Respect the island's tranquility, keep noise to a minimum, and practice leave-no-trace principles.

Let Folegandros Become Your Outdoor Playground

Folegandros is not just a place to visit, it's a place to experience with all your senses, especially outdoors. Whether you're conquering rocky trails, diving into hidden coves, sailing along a sunlit coast, or simply breathing deeply in a quiet grove, the island invites you to slow down and connect. These outdoor adventures blend exercise, discovery, culture, and peace into a perfect harmony, reminding me why I keep returning here, season after season.

So, pack your hiking shoes, your swimsuit, and an open heart. The island's wild beauty awaits.

Chapter 10: Culture, Traditions & Local Life - Embracing the Heartbeat of Folegandros

Traveling is not just about places; it's about people, their stories, customs, and ways of life. In Folegandros, the island's soul reveals itself through traditions carefully preserved over centuries, communal celebrations filled with laughter and song, and everyday moments that connect you with a timeless rhythm. As someone who's wandered its winding streets and shared countless cups of coffee with locals, I can tell you that immersing yourself in the island's culture transforms your visit from sightseeing into belonging.

This chapter invites you to step beyond the postcards and into the vibrant local life, where every gesture, festival, melody, and historic site holds a piece of Folegandros' unique identity. Together, we'll explore practical cultural insights, the warmth of its traditions, and the treasures of its history that enrich your journey beyond the surface.

10.1 Cultural Etiquette & Island Way of Life

Living Like a Local: Respect and Rhythm

One of the first things I noticed about Folegandros is how deeply the islanders cherish respect for their land, their neighbors, and their customs. The island's pace is unhurried, reflecting a way of life tied to the sun, the sea, and community ties that stretch back generations.

Key Etiquette Tips to Blend In Smoothly:

- **Greetings Matter:** When meeting locals, a warm "Kalimera" (good morning) or "Kalispera" (good evening) goes a long way. Folegandrians are friendly but reserved, so polite greetings open doors.

- **Dress Respectfully:** While beachwear is fine at the shore, cover shoulders and knees when visiting churches or villages; this is a mark of respect.

- **Quiet and Courtesy:** The island values tranquility, especially in residential areas and during siesta hours (typically 2–5 pm). Keep noise levels down and avoid rushing; patience is part of the charm here.

- **Supporting Local Economy:** Buying from family-run shops, artisan markets, or tavernas helps preserve the island's traditions. I always seek out homemade products, like honey, cheeses, or embroidery, that tell a story.

- **Community Connection:** Don't hesitate to ask questions or show genuine interest in local life. Folegandrians appreciate curiosity and openness and may share fascinating stories or invite you for a coffee.

A Day in the Life:

Picture this, early morning, you hear the clatter of bakery trays and smell fresh bread baking in a stone oven. The village slowly awakens; elders sit at the kafeneio (coffee shop), discussing news while sipping Greek coffee. Children play in quiet alleys, and fishermen prepare nets. This is everyday Folegandros, where life unfolds in rhythms older than time, inviting you to slow down and savor each moment.

10.2 Religious Festivals & Local Celebrations

When Tradition Lights Up the Island

Folegandros' calendar is punctuated by vibrant religious festivals and celebrations, each a spectacular display of faith, community, and joy. If you time your visit right, you'll be swept up in these lively events that reveal the island's soul in full color.

Not-to-Miss Festivals:

- **Panagia Festival (August 15):** The island's most important religious holiday honors the Virgin Mary with church services, processions, and an all-night feast in Chora's main square. Locals and visitors gather to share homemade food, wine, and music beneath a starlit sky. I've found the sense of unity and celebration here truly unforgettable.

- **Easter Week:** Easter in Folegandros is marked by solemn rituals, candlelit midnight masses, and vibrant Sunday feasts. The sound of church bells and the aroma of roasting lamb fill the air, creating a moving blend of reverence and festivity.

- **St. George's Day (April 23):** Celebrated with a smaller but heartfelt gathering, this day includes traditional music, dancing, and local delicacies served in village squares.

- **Local Feasts and Panigyria:** Throughout summer, small villages host "panigyria", festive gatherings combining music, dance, and shared meals. These are perfect for experiencing genuine island hospitality, often accompanied by the lively sound of violin and lute.

Tips for Festival Visitors:

- Dress modestly for religious ceremonies; bring a scarf for women when entering churches.

- Participate respectfully, observe customs, join in dances if invited, and savor local foods offered as hospitality.

- Bring a camera, but also take moments to simply be present and soak in the atmosphere.

10.3 Island Music, Dance & Folk Tales

Echoes of the Past in Song and Story

Folegandros' culture pulses through its music, dance, and storytelling traditions, threads that connect the present to generations past. I've often found myself entranced by the haunting melodies and rhythmic dances that fill village squares during evening gatherings.

Musical Heritage:

- The island's music blends influences from the broader Cyclades with its own unique style. The lyra (a small bowed instrument) and the laouto (a long-necked lute) provide a rich, soulful sound. These instruments accompany folk songs that tell tales of love, sea voyages, and island life.

- Traditional songs are often performed during panigyria or informal gatherings, and listening to locals sing these a cappella or with minimal accompaniment is a powerful experience.

Dance Traditions:

- The Syrtos and Kalamatianos are popular Greek dances on the island, involving linked hands and rhythmic steps that create a sense of unity and joy. Visitors are often invited to join, making it a wonderful way to connect.

- Watching elder villagers gracefully lead the dances, passing down steps to younger generations, reveals a living tradition.

Folk Tales and Legends:

- Stories of the sea, pirates, and ancient gods ripple through local lore. One favorite tells of the island's protector saints who kept villagers safe during storms and raids.

- I recommend asking locals for these tales, they're often shared with great pride and humor, adding depth to your understanding of the island.

10.4 Museums, Churches & Historical Highlights

Journey Through Time

To appreciate Folegandros fully, you must walk through its history. The island's museums, churches, and landmarks are quiet keepers of stories, art, and architecture that reveal layers of past civilizations, faith, and community life.

Must-Visit Historical Sites:

- **Panagia Church (Chora):** This iconic whitewashed church with blue domes overlooks the main square and stands as a beacon of island faith. Its simple beauty and serene atmosphere make it a must-see.

- **Church of Agios Georgios:** Located atop a hill, this church offers breathtaking views and is a pilgrimage site during St. George's Day. The walk up is an experience in itself, with olive groves and wildflowers lining the path.

- **Folegandros Folklore Museum:** A small but rich museum showcasing traditional costumes, tools, and household items. Visiting here provides insight into everyday island life from past centuries.

- **Castle of Chora:** The Venetian castle ruins, perched above the village, offer panoramic views and a glimpse into the island's strategic past. I love exploring the narrow alleys within the castle walls, imagining the lives once lived there.

Tips for History Buffs:

- Combine visits with guided tours or audio guides to deepen your knowledge.

- Respect all sites, especially churches, by dressing modestly and maintaining quiet.

- Visit early in the day or late afternoon for the best light and fewer crowds.

Let Culture Be Your Compass

Folegandros is more than stunning vistas and crystal waters, it's a living mosaic of traditions, music, faith, and warm human connections. By embracing the island's cultural etiquette, joining in its vibrant festivals, listening to its ancient songs, and wandering through its historical landmarks, you'll move beyond being a visitor to becoming a part of its ongoing story.

Chapter 11: Seasonal Travel Guide - Discovering Folegandros Through the Year

Visiting Folegandros is like stepping into a living postcard, one that changes its colors and moods with the seasons. As someone who has wandered these winding paths over many years, I've come to appreciate how each season offers its own unique charm, revealing different layers of the island's personality. Whether you seek the wild blooms of spring, the lively festivals of summer, the golden calm of autumn, or the peaceful solitude of winter, Folegandros rewards every traveler with unforgettable moments.

In this chapter, we'll journey through the seasons together, sharing practical tips, cultural insights, and my personal favorite experiences to help you time your visit perfectly and make the most of what this enchanting island has to offer year-round.

11.1 Visiting in Spring: Wildflowers & Serenity

Spring on Folegandros feels like a gentle awakening, where the island bursts into color and the air is filled with fresh scents of thyme, oregano, and wildflowers. It's my absolute favorite time to visit if you crave a peaceful escape away from the summer crowds.

What to Expect:

- **Nature's Palette:** The hills and valleys carpet themselves in vibrant reds, yellows, purples, and whites. Walking the coastal paths or hiking up to the Monastery of Panagia is like stepping into a watercolor painting alive with the fragrance of blooming flowers.

- **Mild Weather:** Daytime temperatures hover comfortably around 17-22°C (63-72°F), perfect for long strolls or exploring villages without breaking a sweat.

- **Calm and Quiet:** Most tavernas and shops begin reopening in April, so the island feels welcoming but still unhurried. You can enjoy authentic interactions with locals without the buzz of tourist crowds.

Practical Tips:

- **Clothing:** Layered outfits work best, and cool mornings give way to pleasantly warm afternoons. Comfortable walking shoes are a must for hiking trails covered in blossoms.

- **Events:** Easter celebrations in spring are deeply moving here. Try to experience a midnight mass or local procession for a true taste of island spirituality.

- **Wildlife & Photography:** Early morning and late afternoon are magical times for birdwatching and capturing the soft golden light on blooming landscapes.

My Recommendation: Pack a picnic and head to Livadaki Beach early in the morning. The spring tranquility and the sea's turquoise shimmer will make you feel like you have a secret piece of paradise all to yourself.

11.2 Summer on the Island: Festivities & Warm Waters

Summer on Folegandros is vibrant and alive, a time when the island's soul shines brightest under the radiant sun. Having spent many summers here, I can tell you the energy is contagious, yet the island never loses its relaxed Cycladic charm.

What to Expect:

- **Sun-Drenched Days:** Temperatures climb to 28-33°C (82-91°F), inviting beach days on crystal-clear waters. Popular spots like Agali and Katergo fill with swimmers and snorkelers basking in warm waves.

- **Festivals & Music:** Summer nights are the heartbeat of Folegandros, especially during the Feast of Panagia (August 15). Streets fill with music, dance, and communal feasts, an intoxicating blend of devotion and celebration.

- **Bustling Villages:** Chora's whitewashed alleys come alive with open-air cafes, artisan shops, and lively chatter. The island's restaurants serve fresh seafood caught that day, paired with local wine.

Practical Tips:

- **Accommodation:** Book early to secure the best rooms, especially near Chora or the beachfront. Options range from cozy guesthouses to boutique hotels with infinity pools.

- **Transport:** Rent a scooter or ATV to explore hidden coves like Livadaki and Faros. Be prepared for occasional crowded ferries during peak season.

- **Etiquette:** Respect local customs by dressing modestly when visiting churches during festivals. Join in dances if invited, you'll find Folegandrians welcoming and warm.

My Recommendation: After a day of swimming, settle into a seaside taverna in Agali for fresh grilled octopus and a chilled glass of Assyrtiko wine. As the sun sets, let the sound of bouzouki music and laughter carry you into a perfect summer night.

11.3 Autumn Escapes: Quiet Shores & Culinary Delights

Autumn on Folegandros is a season of golden light and slower rhythms. This is when the island reveals its more introspective side, making it ideal for travelers seeking tranquility combined with rich culinary experiences.

What to Expect:

- **Cooling Temperatures:** Daytime highs settle around 20-25°C (68-77°F), perfect for hiking, biking, or leisurely exploring villages.

- **Harvest Time:** Olive groves are heavy with fruit, and local producers press fresh olive oil. The vineyards are ripe, and wine tastings become a cherished ritual.

- **Empty Beaches:** Beaches become your own private retreats again, with the sea still warm enough for swimming well into October.

Practical Tips:

- **Food:** Autumn is harvest season, so indulge in freshly pressed olive oil, wild greens, mushrooms, and chestnuts at family-run tavernas. Try "houmous" with local herbs or "gavros" (fried anchovies) with lemon.

- **Events:** Check local calendars for village panigyria, small festivals celebrating saints with traditional music and food.

- **Transportation:** Car and scooter rentals are readily available with no rush or crowds. Walking tours in cooler weather are especially enjoyable.

My Recommendation: Don't miss a visit to the charming village of Ano Meria, where you can explore the Folklore Museum and taste homemade cheeses. End your day with a glass of red wine overlooking the valley's sunset hues, pure magic.

11.4 Winter in Folegandros: Peaceful, Slow, and Authentic

Winter on Folegandros is for the traveler who seeks solitude, reflection, and a genuine connection to island life. I've visited several times in this off-season and found a rare peace that contrasts with the lively summer vibe.

What to Expect:

- **Quiet Villages:** Many tourist facilities close, but the heart of the island, the locals, remain. Chora's cobbled streets are peaceful, and the slow rhythm of daily life invites you to breathe deeply.

- **Mild, Crisp Weather:** Temperatures range from 10-16°C (50-61°F). Rain is more frequent, but sunny days offer crisp, clear skies perfect for hiking.

- **Authentic Encounters:** With fewer tourists, you have the chance to experience Folegandros as locals do, sharing stories in a kafeneio, enjoying freshly baked bread, or watching the sea from a quiet cliff.

Practical Tips:

- **Accommodation:** Many guesthouses offer winter rates and a cozy atmosphere with fireplaces. It's wise to contact places ahead as options may be limited.

- **Transportation:** Public buses run less frequently. Renting a car is advisable for exploring the island fully.

- **Dining:** Some tavernas remain open year-round. Ask locals for recommendations to find hidden gems serving traditional winter dishes like lamb stew and "revithada" (chickpea soup).

My Personal Recommendation: Embrace the quiet with a long hike from Chora to the Church of Agios Georgios, followed by a warm meal at a village taverna. The winter sunsets here are some of the most stunning I've ever witnessed, intense colors reflected off the sea, with the world hushed around you.

Choose Your Season, Find Your Folegandros

Every season on Folegandros paints the island in different hues and moods, inviting travelers to experience its beauty and spirit in distinct ways. Whether you seek springtime blossoms and solitude, summer's festive energy and warm seas, autumn's golden tranquility and flavors, or winter's peaceful authenticity, this island welcomes you with open arms.

Use this guide to plan your visit in harmony with the season that speaks to you most, and prepare to create memories that will linger long after you leave these Cycladic shores.

Chapter 12: Curated Itineraries - Exploring Folegandros One Perfect Day at a Time

Folegandros, though small in size, unfolds like a carefully wrapped gift, layer by layer, moment by moment. With every visit, I've discovered new corners of charm, whether it's an abandoned stone path leading to a forgotten church or a café terrace offering the most glorious sunset view in the Cyclades. In this chapter, I'll guide you through a set of thoughtfully curated itineraries that cater to different travel styles, from whirlwind visits to luxurious escapes. These plans are born of experience and tailored for immersion, ensuring that no matter how long you stay, you'll feel the essence of Folegandros.

12.1 One-Day Highlights Tour

If you've only got 24 hours on the island, don't worry, Folegandros knows how to leave a lasting impression.

Morning:

- **Start in Chora**: Wander the whitewashed alleys just after sunrise, when the town is hushed and bathed in golden light.

Grab a Greek coffee and bougatsa (custard pastry) at Pounta Café overlooking the cliff.

- **Monastery of Panagia**: Hike up the zigzagging path from Chora. The view from the top offers panoramic vistas of the Aegean that will etch themselves into your memory.

Afternoon:

- **Agali Beach**: Catch a local bus or rent a scooter to reach this turquoise haven. Swim, sunbathe, and have a light lunch at Taverna Agali, where the grilled calamari is unforgettable.

- **Katergo Beach (Optional)**: For the adventurous, take a short boat ride from Karavostasis port to this stunning, secluded beach.

Evening:

- **Sunset in Chora**: Head back and find a table at Bezantino, one of my favorite tavernas, for a classic Greek dinner, moussaka, local wine, and friendly chatter with locals and fellow travelers.

- **Nightcap**: End your day with a glass of rakomelo (raki with honey and spices) at BaRaki, a cozy bar tucked into a narrow alley.

12.2 Classic 3-Day Getaway

Perfect for a long weekend, this itinerary gives you a well-rounded taste of Folegandros.

Day 1 – Culture & Cliffs

- Morning in Chora exploring artisan shops.
- Visit the Folklore Museum in Ano Meria.
- Dinner at To Zimaraki, try the handmade pasta with tomato and caper sauce.

Day 2 – Sun & Sea

- Morning swim at Livadi Beach, followed by a boat tour to Katergo.
- Afternoon hike to Chrysospilia Cave (note: check local guides for safe access).
- Sunset picnic on the cliffs with supplies from the local bakery and grocery.

Day 3 – Slow Life & Local Flavor

- Breakfast at your guesthouse, followed by a walk through Petousis, a less-visited rural path.

- Enjoy a traditional meal at Irini's Taverna, with fava, ntakos salad, and goat stew.

- Depart with a heart full of memories and maybe a bottle of local wine in your bag.

12.3 Ultimate 7-Day Island Immersion

For those lucky enough to stay a week, this plan lets you settle into island life.

Day 1: Arrival, orientation walk in Chora, sunset at Panagia.

Day 2: Beach day at Agios Nikolaos, accessible by foot or boat.

Day 3: Day trip to Ano Meria, with a stop at the Ecological and Folklore Museum.

Day 4: Hike from Chora to Livadaki Beach, picnic and stargazing on return.

Day 5: Boat tour of the southern coast, swim in secret coves.

Day 6: Free day to revisit your favorite spots or indulge in a spa session at a luxury hotel.

Day 7: Farewell brunch and slow goodbyes.

Insider tip: Schedule a cooking class with a local home cook, many guesthouses can arrange this for you.

12.4 Family Adventure Itinerary

Folegandros isn't just for couples and solo travelers; it's a wonderland for families, too.

Day 1: Orientation in Chora, gelato at The Loaf, and early dinner.
Day 2: Easy beach day at Agali, calm waters perfect for kids.
Day 3: Visit a working farm near Ano Meria, many offer tours for children.
Day 4: Treasure hunt around Chora's main square.
Day 5: Boat ride and beach games at Vardia Beach near the port.
Meals: Most tavernas offer child-friendly options, ask for soutzoukakia (Greek meatballs), and avoid spicy dishes unless the kids are adventurous.
Where to Stay: Choose a family-run pension or villa with kitchenettes and easy beach access.

12.5 Romantic Escape for Couples

Folegandros was made for romance, sunsets, solitude, and soulful conversations.

Highlights:

- Private picnic at Kastros Hill, overlooking the sea.
- Couples massage at Anemi Hotel Spa.

- Dinner under the stars at Blue Cuisine with fine wines and poetic views.
- Sunrise swim at Serfiotiko Beach, often deserted in the early hours.

Suggested Romantic Spots:

- Church of Panagia at dusk.
- Secret paths behind Chora leading to cliffside benches.
- Rooftop dining at a boutique hotel, ask locals for hidden terrace options.

12.6 Budget Explorer's Plan

Folegandros can be surprisingly affordable if you know where to look.

Stay: Opt for guesthouses in Karavostasis or Ano Meria. Rooms can go as low as €40–50 per night in shoulder seasons.

Eat:

- Breakfast from bakeries (tiropita and coffee under €4).
- Lunches of gyros or Greek sandwiches from Piatsa.
- Dinners at Melissa's or Pounta's offer budget-friendly menus with generous portions.

Activities:

- Free hiking trails crisscross the island.
- Beaches are open-access, carry snacks and reusable bottles.
- Visit churches and viewpoints for memorable, cost-free experiences.

Tip: Visit in May or late September for lower prices and mild weather.

12.7 Exclusive Luxury Experience

If your ideal holiday involves indulgence, Folegandros delivers elegance without crowds.

Stay:

- Anemi Hotel offers minimalist luxury, private pools, and fine dining.
- Blue Sand Boutique Hotel is another superb choice for personalized service and sea views.

Experiences:

- Private boat charter for sunset sailing and island hopping.
- Helicopter transfers from Santorini or Athens for ease and flair.

- Fine dining at Papalagi Seafood, the chef's tasting menu is exquisite.

Wellness:

- Book a yoga session on the beach.
- Schedule a couples massage with sea salt scrubs and aromatherapy.

Exclusive Recommendations:

- Wine-pairing dinners featuring Cycladic varieties.
- Private guided tour of Ano Meria's agricultural history with lunch at a farmstead.

Crafting Your Perfect Journey

Whatever your travel rhythm, fast-paced adventurer, slow walker, budget seeker, or luxury lover, Folegandros bends to match it, all the while offering its own quiet magic. These curated itineraries are just starting points. Once your feet hit the cobbled paths and your eyes take in the endless blue, the island will start guiding you in its own gentle way. Let these plans be your compass, but don't be afraid to wander off-script. After all, some of the best travel stories begin when we get just a little bit lost.

Chapter 13: Island Hopping & Excursions - Adventures Beyond the Horizon

There's something utterly liberating about being on a Greek island, feeling the wind tousle your hair, the salt drying on your skin, and the horizon promising new discoveries just across the water. From Folegandros, the Aegean becomes your playground. Whether you're looking to hop over to nearby gems like Milos, Santorini, and Sikinos or stay local and explore hidden coves by boat, this chapter is your guide to crafting unforgettable days at sea and in the hills. I've sailed these waters, picnicked on deserted beaches, and wandered ancient paths far from the crowds. Let me show you how to do the same.

13.1 Day Trips to Milos, Santorini & Sikinos

Though Folegandros has a magnetic charm that makes it hard to leave, you're just a short ferry or boat ride away from some of the Aegean's most iconic islands.

Milos: A Mosaic of Natural Wonders

Known for its moon-like landscapes and technicolor cliffs, Milos is a geologist's dream and a beach lover's paradise.

I always recommend catching an early ferry from Folegandros (about 1.5–2 hours) and spending the day hopping from one surreal beach to another.

- **Must-see:** Sarakiniko Beach, a dazzling white volcanic landscape that looks like it belongs on another planet.
- **Don't miss:** The catacombs of Milos, among the oldest in the world, and the quiet fishing village of Klima with its colorful boat garages.
- **Travel tip:** Rent a car or ATV upon arrival. Public transport is limited, and many beaches are best accessed by wheels or water taxi.

Santorini: Drama in Every View

Yes, Santorini is popular, but with good reason. I often advise travelers to skip the most crowded times (midday in July and August) and opt for a spring or fall visit instead. Ferries between Folegandros and Santorini take about an hour, making a day trip possible, though you'll likely wish you had more time.

- **Top sights:** The caldera view from Oia, the ancient ruins of Akrotiri, and the black sand beach at Perissa.
- **Gastronomic pleasures:** Grab lunch with a view at Metaxi Mas or sip Assyrtiko wine in a cliffside vineyard.

- **Local insight:** Many overlook the traditional village of Pyrgos, but it offers panoramic views with a fraction of the crowds.

Sikinos: Tranquility Defined

Often bypassed, Sikinos is my secret island love affair. Just 30 minutes by ferry from Folegandros, this sleepy island offers a step back in time and a perfect counterbalance to Folegandros' dramatic cliffs.

- **Highlights:** Visit the Zoodochos Pigi Monastery and stroll the unhurried alleys of Chora.
- **Experience:** Join a wine tasting at the Manalis Winery perched high above the sea.
- **Ideal for:** Travelers craving peace, authenticity, and sunsets without applause.

13.2 Boat Excursions Around Folegandros

There's no better way to understand Folegandros' wild beauty than by circling it by sea. Many of the island's most awe-inspiring spots are inaccessible by road, and all the more magical because of it.

Full-Day and Half-Day Cruises

Several local operators offer boat tours that depart from Karavostasis. I always advise checking weather conditions first, as the Aegean can turn from docile to dramatic quickly.

- **South Coast Route:** This itinerary is my favorite. You'll cruise past sheer cliffs, sea caves, and pristine beaches, stopping at:
    - **Katergo Beach**: Accessible only by boat or footpath, this remote stretch of pebbled bliss is ideal for snorkeling.
    - **Galifos and Agios Nikolaos**: Both are perfect for leisurely swims and shaded lunches under tamarisk trees.
- **Lunch on board:** Most captains offer homemade meze, fresh bread, olives, and local wine, a picnic with a view, bobbing gently in the blue.

Sunset Sailing

For couples or solo wanderers craving beauty and solitude, book a sunset cruise. As the sky transforms into a watercolor painting, you'll watch Chora light up like a lantern clinging to the cliffs. Bring a shawl and your camera, and let the silence soak in.

- **Luxury options:** Some tours offer private charters with champagne and seafood platters.

- **Budget-friendly tip:** Join a shared cruise; the camaraderie of fellow travelers often adds to the magic.

13.3 Scenic Picnics & Off-the-Grid Spots

Sometimes, the most unforgettable excursions don't involve a timetable or a ticket, they just require a sense of adventure and a good pair of walking shoes. Folegandros is crisscrossed with stone-paved paths that lead to intimate, windswept moments few ever find.

Picnic Above the World: Church of Panagia

Even if you've visited Panagia Church before, I recommend returning with a picnic at dusk. Pick up local delicacies, goat cheese, olives, figs, and a bottle of sweet rakomelo, and ascend the zigzag path just before sunset. Lay a blanket beside the church and watch the island shimmer below.

- **What to pack:** A reusable tote, chilled water, a beach towel, and a light sweater.

- **Respect the space:** It's still a place of worship, keep music and voices low.

The Hidden Path to Livadaki Beach

Not for the faint of heart, the trail to Livadaki rewards the determined with one of the most secluded beaches on the island. You'll traverse thyme-scented hillsides, see goats scrambling on terraces, and eventually reach a sliver of sand lapped by emerald water.

- Start from Ano Meria, and allow 45–60 minutes for the descent.
- **Pro tip:** Go early, and bring everything you need; there's no shade, no taverna, and no cell service.

Cave of Chrysospilia: The Mysterious Excursion

This sea cave on the northeast coast is shrouded in myth and largely inaccessible, though some private boat tours can get you close enough to marvel at its size and the historic inscriptions etched into its walls. It was once a place of ancient rituals, and even now, it feels charged with something ancient and sacred.

- **Note:** Entry is currently restricted for conservation, but viewing from the sea is permitted with a knowledgeable guide.

Where the Map Ends, Magic Begins

Island hopping and excursions around Folegandros aren't just about moving from place to place, they're about rediscovering awe in every horizon. Whether you're sailing toward the volcanic shores of Milos, tucking into olives on a hidden cliff, or watching the stars from a deck at sea, you're not just passing through the Aegean, you're becoming part of its story.

Pack your curiosity, stay flexible with the wind, and trust in the unplanned.

Chapter 14: Nightlife & After Dark - The Soul of Folegandros at Twilight

When the sun begins its slow descent behind Folegandros' craggy cliffs, the island seems to inhale, pause, and exhale a different kind of magic. By day, Folegandros stuns with its sun-drenched landscapes and cliffside panoramas, but after dark, a softer, more mysterious side of the island reveals itself. This chapter is a celebration of those dusky hours and midnight moments, from sipping cocktails as the sky blushes pink to wandering candlelit alleys or lying under the stars with nothing but the sound of the wind in your ears.

Let me take you beyond the beach and into the night, where Folegandros glows in a different light.

14.1 Sunset Bars & Rooftop Lounges

Few places in the world can boast sunsets as emotive as those in Folegandros. Here, twilight isn't simply a time of day, it's a ritual. It's when locals and visitors alike pause to admire the Aegean blaze in molten gold before succumbing to indigo night.

And what better way to enjoy this spectacle than with a glass in hand and a breeze on your skin?

Pounta Café: The Golden Hour Favorite

Tucked into the upper reaches of Chora, Pounta Café is my perennial recommendation for first-time visitors. From its stone terrace, you'll feel like you're floating above the world. As the sun dips behind the horizon, casting a fiery glow over the sea, the vibe here is chilled yet charged with quiet reverence.

- **Try this:** Their signature cocktail with mastiha and fresh citrus, refreshing, aromatic, uniquely Greek.

- **Insider tip:** Arrive at least 30 minutes before sunset to snag a front-row seat.

Astarti Bar: Where Elegance Meets Island Vibe

For those seeking a more refined ambiance, Astarti offers a polished rooftop experience. This is the spot where local wine lovers and cocktail aficionados mingle beneath string lights. The music is low and curated, the views stretch over the village rooftops to the endless sea, and the staff know their craft.

- **What to order:** An Assyrtiko wine spritz or a cucumber-gin infusion with herbs plucked from the bar's own rooftop garden.

- **Good to know:** The dress code is relaxed but stylish, this is the time to trade flip-flops for espadrilles.

Budget-Friendly Chill: Beez Cocktail Bar

Tucked just off the main square in Chora, Beez offers a casual yet creative take on island nightlife. It's cozy, colorful, and perfect for travelers who prefer boho charm to glam. The bartenders here are generous with their pours, and their playlist is as eclectic as the guests.

- **Don't miss:** Their passion fruit mojito or a shot of local rakomelo as a digestif.
- **Travel tip:** During peak season, expect it to buzz with energy until the early hours.

14.2 Live Music & Cultural Nights

Folegandros may not throb with the thumping beats of Mykonos, but its nights are far from dull. Here, music and culture are part of the island's DNA, flowing naturally into village squares, stone amphitheaters, and tucked-away tavernas.

Open-Air Concerts in Chora

In the summer months, the main square in Chora transforms into an open-air stage.

It's not uncommon to stumble upon a folk music performance, complete with lute players and dancers in traditional Cycladic dress. One balmy August evening, I found myself clapping along with strangers and locals alike, drawn into a spontaneous circle dance beneath the stars.

- **Look for:** Event posters on the notice boards in Chora and Ano Meria.

- **Cultural etiquette:** Participation is encouraged, but be respectful, applaud the performers, and ask before joining dances.

Tavernas with Live Music

A few tavernas offer live Greek music a few nights a week. One of my favorites is I Piatsa in Chora, where bouzouki and vocals echo through the narrow alleyways while guests dine on lamb stewed with capers and honey-drenched figs.

- **Pair your meal with:** A carafe of house wine and a slice of melopita (honey pie) for dessert.

- **Best nights to go:** Fridays and Saturdays, though it's wise to ask the staff in advance.

Cultural Festivals & Religious Feasts

If you're lucky enough to visit during a local festival, you're in for a treat. Celebrations like the feast of the Virgin Mary (August 15th) are marked with candle processions, music, communal meals, and fireworks that light up the cliffs.

- **Traveler tip:** These festivals offer rare access to authentic local traditions. Be respectful, dress modestly, and embrace the hospitality.

14.3 Stargazing & Quiet Evenings in Nature

For many, the most memorable nights in Folegandros aren't the ones spent in bars or concerts, but in nature, in stillness, under a dome of stars. The island's minimal light pollution and sweeping, elevated landscapes make it a natural observatory.

Church of Panagia: A Celestial Viewpoint

Long after the sunset crowds have departed, the path to the Church of Panagia offers solitude and silence. Bring a flashlight, climb the switchback trail, and settle into a perch above the sea. The constellations here feel close enough to touch.

- **What to bring:** A blanket or sarong to lie on, a thermos of herbal tea or a small flask of tsipouro, and perhaps a book of Greek myths.

- **Note:** Watch your step on the descent, it can be tricky in the dark.

Agali Beach at Night

Agali may be lively by day, but by night it's a haven for moonlit swims and quiet reflection. I've spent evenings here wrapped in a light jacket, listening to the gentle rhythm of the tide and tracing shooting stars across the sky.

- **Best during:** New moons, when the Milky Way glows brightest.
- **Safety tip:** Always go with someone and check tide conditions beforehand.

Camping Under the Stars: Livadaki & Ambeli

If you're the adventurous sort, consider a night of rustic stargazing at one of the island's remote beaches. Livadaki and Ambeli are favorites among free spirits and nature lovers. While wild camping is technically not allowed, many sleep beneath the stars with just a blanket and a beach mat. Just be discreet, leave no trace, and respect the land.

The Quiet Pulse of Folegandros Nights

Nightfall on Folegandros isn't about neon lights or nightclub lines, it's about soft music, heartfelt conversations, ancient rituals, and the rhythms of nature. It's where the day's intensity melts into a kind of dreamscape, where you can dance in a square, sip wine on a rooftop, or simply gaze upward and get lost in infinity.

As you plan your nights on the island, lean into the slower pace. Let the moonlight guide you down cobbled paths. Say yes to the late-night serenade or the unexpected shot of ouzo from a new friend. Here, the night doesn't demand anything from you, it invites you to simply be.

Chapter 15: Travel Tips & Safety - Navigating Folegandros with Confidence

There's something freeing about stepping off a ferry onto a sun-splashed island like Folegandros, where the pace slows and the beauty is everywhere. But as serene as it may seem, even a slice of paradise benefits from a bit of preparation. Over the years of visiting Folegandros, I've gathered a wealth of practical knowledge, some hard-earned, others shared over ouzo with locals, that can help you avoid pitfalls, travel safely, and get the most out of your time on the island.

Whether you're here for a romantic escape, a family holiday, or a solo soul-searching retreat, these tips will serve as your invisible safety net, keeping you informed, empowered, and ready for anything.

15.1 Local Laws & Traveler Rights

Folegandros, like the rest of Greece, is governed by a legal system that respects both locals and visitors, but it's essential to understand the local laws so you can travel respectfully and avoid misunderstandings.

Respecting Greek Culture and Legal Norms

- Dress modestly at churches and religious sites. Shoulders and knees should be covered, carry a scarf or shawl if you're unsure.

- Alcohol is legal and freely available, but public intoxication, especially disorderly conduct, is frowned upon and can lead to fines or police involvement.

- Drugs are strictly illegal. Even small quantities can result in serious legal consequences.

- Smoking laws prohibit smoking in indoor public places, though enforcement can vary.

Traveler Rights You Should Know

- You have the right to request receipts in shops, taxis, and restaurants. It's also a good way to ensure you're not being overcharged.

- In case of disputes (e.g., with rental agencies), you can seek help from the Hellenic Tourism Organization (EOT).

- EU citizens can use their EHIC cards for healthcare access, while others should ensure they have proper travel insurance coverage.

15.2 Avoiding Common Pitfalls & Scams

Folegandros is remarkably safe compared to major tourist hubs in Europe. Still, small oversights can lead to unnecessary stress. Here are the most common mistakes and how to sidestep them.

Transportation Mishaps

- Scooter and ATV rentals are popular, but insurance coverage is often limited. Always check the fine print, inspect the vehicle thoroughly, and take photos of any damage before driving off.

- Buses are reliable, but don't assume they run late into the night; check schedules ahead of time.

Overpaying at Restaurants or Shops

- Avoid restaurants with aggressive "menu pushers" in touristy areas. The best places often let their food speak for itself.

- Confirm prices before ordering off-menu or selecting fresh seafood, as some items are charged by weight.

Accommodation Surprises

- Not all "sea view" listings are created equal. I once booked a room labeled "panoramic sea views" only to find a sliver of ocean visible through the bathroom window. Read reviews carefully and look for real guest photos.

Money Matters

- Many establishments still prefer cash, especially in Ano Meria and remote tavernas. While ATMs are available, it's smart to carry enough euros for small purchases.

- Watch out for hidden foreign transaction fees if using international cards. Notify your bank before traveling.

15.3 Emergency Numbers & Medical Access

It's a good idea to keep vital numbers handy, just in case. Folegandros is small, and the community is tight-knit, so help is usually close at hand.

Essential Emergency Contacts

- **General Emergency (Police, Fire, Ambulance):** 112
- **Local Police Station (Chora):** +30 22860 41249
- **Municipal Health Center (Chora):** +30 22860 41204

- **Pharmacy (Chora):** +30 22860 41333

Medical Care on the Island

Folegandros has a basic but well-staffed Health Center in Chora, which handles minor emergencies and general care. For more complex medical issues, patients are transferred by boat or helicopter to Santorini or Athens.

- **Pro tip:** Travel insurance that covers emergency evacuation is well worth the investment.

- **Pharmacy tip:** Many medications are available over-the-counter in Greece. Just describe your symptoms, and the pharmacist will assist.

15.4 Health, Safety & Solo Travel Considerations

Even in a peaceful destination like Folegandros, your safety and well-being should never be taken for granted. Solo travelers in particular should take a few extra precautions.

Staying Healthy in the Heat

- Always carry water, especially when hiking or exploring remote beaches like Livadaki.

- Wear sun protection, the Aegean sun is intense even in spring and autumn.

- Many local dishes are rich and hearty; if you have dietary restrictions, learn a few key Greek phrases or use a translation app to communicate clearly in tavernas.

Beach & Swimming Safety

- Some beaches, like Agios Nikolaos, are accessible only by foot or boat, plan ahead, and bring sturdy shoes and supplies.

- There are no lifeguards on most beaches. Swim only if you're confident, and avoid rocky areas when the sea is choppy.

Tips for Solo Travelers

- Folegandros is a very safe destination for solo travelers, including women. Locals are welcoming and protective of visitors.

- If hiking solo, let someone know your route, and bring a power bank for your phone.

- Solo diners are warmly received, there's no stigma here about eating alone, and some of my most memorable meals were shared with curious locals who struck up a conversation.

15.5 Travel Apps & Useful Services

Technology can greatly enhance your trip to Folegandros. Here are the tools I always keep at my fingertips.

Navigation & Transit

- **Google Maps** – Reliable for roads and village paths, but hiking trails may be better navigated with apps like:

- **AllTrails** or **Komoot** – Excellent for offline hiking routes.

- **Moovit** – For checking bus routes and ferry schedules (though info can be patchy off-season).

Language & Communication

- **Google Translate** – Download Greek for offline use.

- **Speak & Translate** – Handy for voice-to-voice conversation in tavernas or with older locals who may not speak English.

Weather & Alerts

- **Windy** – Useful for checking wind and sea conditions, especially if you're planning a boat excursion.

- **EMY Weather (Hellenic National Meteorological Service)** – Provides updates during the fire season and alerts during extreme weather.

Local Insights

- **Folegandros App (if available)** – Some years, the island runs a basic app with event listings, beach updates, and local tips. Ask at the tourism office.

Travel Prepared, Travel Free

While Folegandros invites you to surrender to its pace and let go of everyday stress, being a prepared traveler gives you the freedom to fully embrace each moment. Knowing your rights, planning for health and safety, and arming yourself with the right tools transforms your trip from good to extraordinary.

I often say that Folegandros is a place where little goes wrong, but when it does, the island steps in like an old friend. Whether it's a pharmacist who goes out of her way to help or a stranger who walks you back to your pension in the dark, the warmth here is genuine.

Chapter 16: Managing Your Budget - Exploring Folegandros Without Breaking the Bank

One of the reasons I keep coming back to Folegandros is that it rewards travelers of all budgets. Whether you're a backpacker watching every euro or a luxury traveler who enjoys the finer things in life, Folegandros has a way of making you feel like you're getting more than you paid for. The island may not be the cheapest in the Cyclades, but it offers an excellent value-to-experience ratio. And if you know where to look, you'll find a wealth of authentic moments that cost very little, or nothing at all.

This chapter is a guide to doing Folegandros smartly. I've broken it down into what I've learned through dozens of visits, how to handle currency, what to expect for daily costs, and how to enjoy the island fully without draining your bank account.

16.1 Currency, ATMs & Card Use

Greece uses the euro (€), and on Folegandros, cash is still king, especially in smaller villages like Ano Meria and remote beaches where electronic systems are spotty or nonexistent.

Accessing Money on the Island

- There are only a couple of ATMs on the island, located in Chora. They tend to be reliable, but during peak season or festival weekends, they may run out of cash. Always carry enough euros, especially if you're heading to remote areas.

- Many tavernas and shops prefer cash, even if they accept cards. For small purchases like snacks, bottled water, or bus tickets, it's best not to rely on plastic.

- Cards are accepted in mid- to high-end restaurants, boutique hotels, and car rental agencies, but ask before assuming.

Pro Tips for Handling Money

- Withdraw in larger amounts to avoid repeated ATM fees. Greek ATMs often charge a flat fee of €2–3 per withdrawal, regardless of your home bank.

- Notify your bank before traveling to avoid having your card blocked for suspicious activity.

- Use a currency conversion app or travel card with no foreign transaction fees to maximize your exchange rate.

16.2 Daily Costs & Typical Prices

Folegandros is slightly more expensive than some less-touristed Greek islands but remains far more affordable than Santorini or Mykonos. Your daily expenses will depend on your travel style, the season, and how often you indulge in splurges.

Approximate Daily Costs

- **Budget Traveler**: €50–70/day

  Includes hostel or budget room, public bus, local meals, and occasional beach entry fees or drinks.

- **Mid-Range Traveler**: €100–150/day

  Covers boutique accommodation, scooter rental, dinner with wine, entrance to attractions, and a few extras.

- **Luxury Traveler**: €200–400+/day

  Offers stays at high-end hotels, gourmet dining, private excursions, and full-service beach clubs.

Sample Prices

- Coffee at a local café: €2–3
- Simple taverna meal (souvlaki, salad, water): €10–15
- Three-course dinner with wine: €25–40
- Scooter rental (daily): €25–35

- Local bus fare: €2–3 per ride

- Beach umbrella and lounger: €8–12 per day

- Boutique guesthouse (high season): €100–180 per night

- Budget room or studio (off-season): €50–70 per night

Prices tend to spike in July and August, especially around the Feast of the Assumption on August 15th, when Greeks flood the islands. Traveling in shoulder seasons (May–June, September–October) not only saves money but also offers milder weather and a more relaxed atmosphere.

16.3 Budgeting Tips for Every Traveler

Traveling smart on Folegandros doesn't mean cutting corners, it means knowing where to spend and where to save. Here are my go-to strategies for getting the best value from your trip.

Accommodation Hacks

- Book early for high season or travel in the shoulder months for better rates and quieter experiences.

- Consider pensions and family-run studios in Ano Meria or Karavostasis. These places often come with kitchens, allowing you to prepare simple meals.

Transportation Savvy

- The **local bus system** is reliable and incredibly cheap. It connects most major areas and is great for budget travelers.

- If you're planning multiple trips or beach hops, renting a scooter may be more cost-effective than relying on taxis.

Dining on a Dime

- Eat like a local. Stick to traditional tavernas, where portions are generous, and dishes like fava, tomato fritters, and grilled sardines are affordable and delicious.

- Share a few mezze (small plates) with travel companions rather than ordering individual meals.

- Shop at mini-markets for fresh fruit, Greek yogurt, bread, and olives, ideal for beach picnics or breakfast with a view.

Drink Wisely

- House wine and local ouzo are both flavorful and affordable.

- Bring your own water bottle. Tap water is safe to drink in Folegandros, unlike many other islands where bottled water is required.

16.4 Free & Low-Cost Experiences

Some of Folegandros' greatest treasures cost nothing at all. If you're drawn to beauty, history, and nature, as I am, you'll find the island incredibly generous in what it offers without a price tag.

Sunset at the Church of Panagia

The winding path up to Panagia Church, perched high above Chora, offers one of the most breathtaking views on the island. Arrive in time for the golden hour, and watch the Aegean burn orange and lavender, no admission fee, no crowds, just timeless serenity.

Hiking the Old Paths

Folegandros is laced with ancient mule tracks that now serve as scenic hiking trails. My personal favorite? The hike from Ano Meria to Agios Georgios beach, a moderately challenging route with panoramic views and a perfect swimming cove as your reward.

Beach Days

Many of the best beaches, including Katergo, Livadaki, and Agios Nikolaos, are free to access. Bring your own towel, snacks, and snorkel gear for a full day of sea-soaked bliss.

Cultural Events & Panigiria

If you're lucky enough to be on the island during a local festival (panigiri), don't miss it. These celebrations include free food, music, and dancing, a real glimpse into the heart of Greek island life. Dates vary, so ask your host or check the local noticeboards.

Wander & Wonder

Chora, with its labyrinth of whitewashed alleys, hidden chapels, and flowering balconies, is a destination in itself. Get up early to beat the crowds and see the town wake up, bakers carrying trays of warm bread, locals opening shutters, and sleepy cats stretching in the sun.

More Beauty, Less Expense

Folegandros proves that some of the richest travel experiences don't have to come with a luxury price tag. By planning wisely, staying flexible, and embracing the local rhythm, you can savor this enchanting island without overspending. Whether you're sipping strong Greek coffee in a shady square or climbing the cliffside path at sunset, you'll find that the true wealth of Folegandros lies in its atmosphere, authenticity, and simplicity.

Chapter 17: Indulgent Escapes – Luxury Travel in Folegandros

There's a quiet kind of luxury that exists on Folegandros, one that doesn't clamor for attention but whispers elegance in every sun-soaked stone and horizon-tipped cocktail. Unlike the flashier destinations in the Cyclades, Folegandros draws those who prefer understated indulgence: curated comforts, exquisite views, and moments that unfold at their own unhurried pace.

I've always found Folegandros to be a sanctuary for the discerning traveler. Here, luxury isn't about excess; it's about exclusivity, authenticity, and experiences crafted with care. Whether you're lounging in a cliffside suite with an infinity pool, savoring a wine-paired sunset dinner, or chartering a private yacht to a hidden cove, the island offers indulgent escapes for those who know where to look. Let's explore the finest ways to immerse yourself in Folegandros at its most luxurious.

17.1 5-Star Hotels with Infinity Pools

The most luxurious accommodations in Folegandros are perched on the dramatic cliffs of Chora, where the views stretch endlessly across the Aegean, and time seems to slow down.

These are not sprawling resorts but boutique masterpieces, carefully woven into the island's terrain.

Blue Sand Boutique Hotel & Suites

Tucked just above Agali Bay, Blue Sand combines Cycladic charm with modern sophistication. Each suite features minimalist interiors, organic textures, and private terraces, some with outdoor jacuzzis overlooking the sea. The personalized service is impeccable, and breakfast on your balcony, with freshly baked spanakopita and mountain tea, sets a tone of indulgence for the day.

Anemi Hotel

Located near Karavostasis port, Anemi is the island's only official five-star hotel and a favorite among design lovers. The clean lines, stone façades, and curated art collection give it a refined feel. The highlight? It's sea-facing infinity pool, arguably the most photogenic on the island. Relaxing here with a chilled glass of Assyrtiko is pure serenity.

Personal Tip

Request a sunset-facing room, these get booked months in advance, but they reward you with golden hour views that are simply unforgettable. And always ask about in-room spa treatments, they often aren't advertised but can be arranged privately.

17.2 Private Yacht Charters & Helicopter Transfers

There's something unforgettable about seeing Folegandros from the sea, its jagged cliffs plunging into turquoise depths, secret caves glowing in the sunlight. Chartering a private yacht transforms your island stay into a cinematic journey.

Private Yacht Experiences

Several services offer half-day and full-day charters, with captains who know the coastline intimately. These excursions take you to secluded beaches like Livadaki and Vardia, only accessible by boat. Snorkeling in sea caves, diving into crystalline waters, and sipping wine on deck as the sun dips behind Sikinos, this is the stuff of luxury travel dreams.

- Most charters include freshly prepared Greek meze, local wine, and snorkeling gear.
- For couples, ask for a sunset sail, they'll time it perfectly for a romantic champagne toast.

Helicopter Transfers

If you're hopping over from Santorini or Athens and want to bypass ferries, helicopter transfers offer the ultimate in speed and style. While not cheap, they save time and offer unparalleled aerial views of the Cyclades' sun-splashed isles.

- Book well in advance, especially during summer weekends.

- Check with your hotel, many offer concierge services to arrange helicopter landings near Karavostasis or private helipads nearby.

17.3 Fine Dining & Premium Wine Tastings

While Folegandros doesn't have Michelin stars, it boasts a constellation of culinary experiences that rival the best in Greece. Think fresh-caught seafood, heirloom vegetables, and plates painted with olive oil, lemon, and herbs from hillside gardens.

Pounda in Chora

Romantic and refined, Pounda is where I return for special evenings. Dine under bougainvillea-draped pergolas, sampling dishes like octopus carpaccio with citrus zest or lamb slow-cooked in mavrodaphne wine. Their curated wine list includes rare Cycladic vintages. Ask for a sommelier pairing if you want the full experience.

Zefiros Anemos

Perched on the cliffside, Zefiros offers panoramic views with every bite. Their modern twist on classic Greek flavors, such as fennel-scented fish soup or feta mousse with caramelized figs, is pure delight. The restaurant's candlelit ambiance and attentive service elevate the entire evening.

Wine Tastings with a View

Local wine bars in Chora are beginning to offer premium tasting menus showcasing Greek varietals. Assyrtiko, Malagousia, and Xinomavro wines are paired with artisanal cheeses, nuts, and honey from the island. Some vineyards from Santorini even host pop-up tastings during the summer season. Ask around discreetly or check local events listings.

17.4 Spa Days & Private Retreats

After days of exploring sunbaked paths and wind-swept beaches, indulging in wellness feels like both a reward and a reset. Folegandros may be a small island, but it hides some deeply rejuvenating experiences.

In-House Spa Services

Many luxury hotels offer in-room massages, facials, and aromatherapy sessions. Anemi Hotel has a full-service wellness suite, while Blue Sand arranges open-air treatments on private balconies. The signature massage with olive oil and island herbs is my personal favorite, a sensory journey rooted in the land's own essence.

Private Yoga & Meditation

Several retreat guides host one-on-one yoga and meditation sessions at sunrise or sunset, often atop hilltops or beach platforms. Something is grounding about practicing yoga with only the sound of waves and cicadas in your ears.

Luxury Day Passes

Even if you're not staying at a 5-star property, some hotels offer day passes to their pools and spa amenities. This is a great way to enjoy premium comforts without the full price tag of accommodation.

The Art of Subtle Splendor

Luxury on Folegandros isn't loud, it doesn't announce itself in gold or glamour. Instead, it arrives quietly: in a soft breeze on a sun-drenched terrace, in the deep sigh that follows a perfect bite of grilled sea bass, in the hush of your own private cove. This is a destination that rewards those who know that the most indulgent moments are often the most peaceful.

If you're seeking a trip steeped in elegance, authenticity, and curated comfort, Folegandros is a masterpiece waiting to be experienced.

Chapter 18: Guide for Solo Travelers

Traveling alone is more than just a journey, it's a revelation. The rhythm of your footsteps on unfamiliar cobbled streets, the freedom of deciding your day's fate at the breakfast table, and the unparalleled intimacy of experiencing a destination through your own unfiltered lens, solo travel is a poetic pursuit of self and world. And in Folegandros, it feels like the island was designed for exactly this kind of adventure.

Tucked away from the buzz of the more frequented Cycladic destinations, Folegandros offers a unique balance of serenity and sociability. It's quiet without being lonely, charming without being overwhelming, and authentic without being inaccessible. As someone who's wandered this sun-kissed gem alone many times, I can assure you that it's not just a safe place for solo travelers, it's a sanctuary.

Let me walk you through what it's like to explore Folegandros solo, where to go, who to meet, and how to turn your solitude into a rich, memorable experience.

18.1 Is Folegandros Safe for Solo Travel?

Safety is the first question every solo traveler must consider. And here's the simple truth: Folegandros is one of the safest islands in Greece. Its close-knit community, low crime rate, and respectful atmosphere make it ideal for travelers flying solo.

Day or night, I've wandered Chora's narrow alleys with confidence, my camera in hand, never once looking over my shoulder. Whether you're hiking remote trails or enjoying a late-night ouzo in a cliffside bar, you'll rarely encounter any reason to worry.

Tips for staying safe:

- Keep emergency numbers saved in your phone (included in the Travel Tips chapter).

- Inform your hotel if you plan on hiking alone, especially to remote beaches like Livadaki.

- The locals are incredibly kind, don't hesitate to ask for help if you get turned around or need advice.

Insider Insight: Because Folegandros is so small, locals notice and remember visitors. It creates a sense of being looked after, even when you're traveling alone.

18.2 Solo-Friendly Activities & Social Hotspots

Folegandros may be tranquil, but boredom isn't part of the equation. Solo travelers will find a bounty of experiences tailored perfectly to independent exploration, whether you're seeking solitude or moments of serendipitous social connection.

Wander Chora at Golden Hour

Chora is a postcard come to life, whitewashed buildings with blue shutters, blooming bougainvillea, and winding alleys that open onto panoramic terraces. At golden hour, the town glows with a soft, amber hue, and every corner seems to invite a photo or quiet contemplation. Grab a seat at a small café in Pounta Square, order a frappé, and just people-watch.

Hike the Ancient Paths

Folegandros boasts a network of old donkey paths that now serve as hiking trails. As a solo traveler, this is your chance to feel the island's timelessness. My favorite is the trail from Chora to Agios Nikolaos Beach, about a 45-minute walk rewarded with turquoise waters and a rustic beach taverna.

- Start early to avoid the midday heat.
- Carry water and wear sturdy shoes.

- Don't miss the church of Panagia, the path leading up from Chora is steep but offers jaw-dropping views at sunset.

Beach Days for One

Beaches like Katergo and Agkali are quiet and welcoming for solo sunbathers. Bring a book, rent a lounger, and soak in the sound of waves rather than conversation. You'll often find fellow solo travelers doing the same.

Evenings in Chora

At night, the village squares come alive with laughter and clinking glasses. Dine alone without feeling alone, Greek hospitality makes solo diners feel welcome. Try Eva's Garden for grilled seabass and house wine, or Piatsa for hearty moussaka and people-watching.

18.3 Meeting Locals & Other Travelers

Folegandros may be small, but it's wonderfully social in an organic, non-touristy way. If you're open to it, you'll find plenty of opportunities to strike up conversations, often with locals who are proud to share their island or fellow solo travelers craving a friendly chat.

Start with Your Stay

Small boutique hotels and family-run guesthouses tend to foster interaction. Hosts often go out of their way to introduce guests, share local tips, and even invite you to small gatherings or cultural events.

Recommended stays for solo travelers:

- **Vrahos Boutique Hotel** – Intimate and scenic, with a communal breakfast terrace.
- **Polikandia Hotel** – Family-owned, with friendly staff who remember your name by the second day.

Take a Local Cooking Class

Some tavernas offer informal cooking lessons if you ask in advance. Learning to make stuffed vine leaves (dolmadakia) or Folegandros-style matsata (local pasta) is both fun and a great way to meet fellow travelers in a relaxed setting.

Join a Boat Tour

Solo-friendly and naturally social, boat tours around the island introduce you to otherwise inaccessible beaches and scenic spots like Chrysospilia Cave. Shared tours often turn into floating mini-communities, especially when lunch and wine are involved.

Visit a Kafeneio

The island's traditional coffee houses, or kafeneia, are the heartbeat of local life. Don't be shy about sitting down for a Greek coffee and striking up a conversation; many locals speak English, and a friendly "kalimera" goes a long way.

Tips for Embracing the Solo Travel Vibe

- **Learn a few Greek phrases**: Even just greetings and polite expressions will endear you to locals.

- **Bring a journal**: Folegandros inspires reflection. I've filled many pages on terraces overlooking the sea.

- **Go offline**: Signal can be spotty in remote areas. Use it as a chance to disconnect.

- **Be open**: Accept that not every day will be action-packed. Sometimes the beauty of solo travel is simply sitting still.

Finding Yourself on the Edge of the Aegean

Folegandros has a way of making you feel like you're the only person in the world, and yet, never lonely. It's in the silent stretches of cliffside trails, the warm nods from shopkeepers, the shared laughter over meze at a tavern table. Traveling here alone means more than just seeing the island, it means letting it see you.

If you've been hesitant about solo travel, let this be your sign. Pack light, come curious, and allow yourself to slow down. Folegandros is ready to welcome you, not as a stranger, but as someone it's always known was coming.

Chapter 19: Family-Friendly Travel

Family travel is a different kind of adventure, one filled with laughter echoing across sun-drenched coves, sleepy toddlers in strollers after a day of discovery, and the quiet joy of introducing your children to the wonders of the world. On the island of Folegandros, this kind of travel takes on a magical quality. With its safe, walkable villages, uncrowded beaches, and slow, genuine pace of life, it's the perfect destination for families looking to bond, explore, and unwind together.

I've traveled to Folegandros with nieces and nephews in tow, and each trip has been an enriching blend of shared stories, spontaneous picnics by the sea, and memory-making in the most scenic of settings. This chapter is your guide to enjoying the island through a family-friendly lens, whether you're traveling with toddlers, teens, or a multigenerational group.

19.1 Things to Do with Kids

Folegandros is not a theme-park island, and that's its charm. What it offers instead is authentic, hands-on experiences that foster creativity, curiosity, and connection. You won't find roller coasters, but you will find winding paths through whitewashed villages, hidden sea caves, and donkeys grazing along ancient stone walls.

Top family activities:

- **Hiking to Agios Nikolaos Beach:** This scenic 45-minute trail is gentle enough for school-age kids and rewards you with shallow, calm waters and a taverna for snacks and fresh juice.

- **Exploring Chora's car-free alleys:** Safe and stroller-friendly, Chora is a labyrinth of cobbled streets lined with quaint shops, ice cream stands, and hidden courtyards where children can roam freely.

- **Boat excursion around the island:** Take a half-day boat trip that stops at beaches only accessible by water. Most tours provide snorkeling gear, and older kids will love jumping off the boat into turquoise waters.

- **Church of Panagia walk at sunset:** For active families, this uphill path to the iconic white church offers a little challenge and a lot of reward, a sweeping view over the sea that captivates everyone, no matter their age.

Fun and educational moments: Visit the Folegandros Folklore Museum in Ano Meria to introduce kids to how islanders lived before modern tourism. The preserved farmhouse is a time capsule of Cycladic life, complete with traditional tools and cooking equipment.

19.2 Best Family Accommodations

The island's hospitality scene is tailor-made for comfort and relaxation. While Folegandros does lean toward boutique-style accommodations, many properties warmly welcome families with spacious rooms, kitchenettes, pools, and easy access to kid-friendly areas.

Top family-friendly stays:

- **Blue Sand Boutique Hotel & Suites (Agali Beach):** Offers spacious suites with balconies and quick access to the beach. The peaceful surroundings are ideal for families seeking both convenience and tranquility.

- **Polikandia Hotel (Chora):** A family-run gem that treats you like one of their own. The large garden and pool area provide space for kids to unwind after a day of exploring.

- **Anemomilos Apartments:** Self-catering apartments in a quiet part of Chora, great for longer stays. Each unit includes a kitchenette, allowing for easy family meals.

- **Folegandros Apartments:** Centrally located with multi-room options and a delightful pool, this is a perfect home base for families who want to explore Chora without a car.

Insider tip: If traveling with babies or toddlers, consider staying in Chora or Agali for easy access to shops, restaurants, and medical services. Some properties will even provide cribs and high chairs if requested in advance.

19.3 Child-Friendly Beaches & Attractions

Unlike some of the more crowded Greek islands, Folegandros offers calm, unspoiled beaches where children can splash safely and parents can actually relax. The sand is warm, the sea is gentle, and the atmosphere is refreshingly tranquil.

Top beaches for families:

- **Agali Beach:** Arguably the best family beach on the island. It has soft sand, shallow water, and a string of tavernas serving up local dishes and fresh juices. You can rent umbrellas and loungers for shade and comfort.

- **Livadi Beach:** A flat and wide stretch of sand near the port with shallow waters, ideal for toddlers and beach games. Fewer tourists mean plenty of space to spread out and play.

- **Karavostasis (Port Beach):** Surprisingly pleasant and extremely convenient. If you're arriving by ferry or just want a quick splash, this beach has calm surf and shaded spots.

More to explore:

- **Petting donkeys in Ano Meria:** Keep an eye out for the friendly farm animals that often roam near this highland village. Kids love the novelty and photo ops.

- **Evening strolls in Chora:** As the sun sets, families emerge into the gentle buzz of village life. The town squares become playgrounds for local children, and your kids will often make instant friends without a shared language.

19.4 Practical Tips for Traveling with Children

Traveling with children requires preparation, but Folegandros makes it surprisingly smooth with its laid-back nature and helpful locals. Here are some tried-and-true strategies to keep everyone happy and relaxed.

Transportation:

- **Getting around:** The island is compact, and many visitors forgo a car entirely. For families, however, renting a small car can be helpful, especially if you want to visit remote beaches or stay outside of Chora.

- **Public buses:** Regular routes connect Chora with Ano Meria, Agali, and Karavostasis. They're reliable and budget-friendly.

Dining:

- Most tavernas offer simple, kid-friendly food like grilled chicken, pasta, and fresh bread. Greek cuisine is generous and unpretentious, perfect for picky eaters.

- Many restaurants are open-air with relaxed service, so there's no pressure if the little ones get restless.

Health & Safety:

- There is a small pharmacy and medical clinic in Chora, and the locals are quick to help in emergencies.

- Sunscreen and hats are essential, Greek sun is strong, even in shoulder seasons.

- Always carry reusable water bottles; tap water is not recommended for drinking, but bottled water is widely available and inexpensive.

Packing suggestions:

- Swimwear, sandals, and sun protection are essentials.

- A lightweight stroller is handy in Chora and at the port but can be challenging on cobbled or hilly paths.

- Bring snacks for long beach days or hiking trips, as some areas are remote with limited access to shops.

Creating Timeless Memories on Folegandros

Folegandros is not a place that demands an itinerary, it invites you to slow down, breathe in the sea air, and enjoy each moment. As a family destination, it offers something rare: a chance to reconnect with each other in a setting untouched by tourist excess or hurried schedules.

Children will remember the warm stones under their feet, the sound of goats on a hillside trail, the taste of tomatoes ripened by the Aegean sun. Parents will cherish the quiet mornings on shaded terraces, the joy of discovery reflected in their children's eyes, and the peaceful rhythm that permeates every part of island life. Whether it's your first family holiday or one of many, Folegandros will stay with you long after the suitcases are unpacked

Chapter 20: Responsible Travel in Folegandros

Winding through the quiet alleys of Chora or gazing out across the blinding white cliffs above the Aegean, it's easy to believe that Folegandros is untouched. And in many ways, it is. But beneath the pristine vistas and the slowed rhythms of island life, there's a delicate balance at play, one that hinges on the care we bring as visitors. Responsible travel isn't just a trend here; it's a commitment to protecting a cultural and natural heritage that has endured for centuries.

As someone who has visited Folegandros time and again, I've learned that traveling responsibly here means listening to the land, honoring the people, and treading lightly. In this chapter, I'll guide you through the many ways you can immerse yourself in the island's beauty while ensuring it remains just as enchanting for future generations.

20.1 How to Travel Sustainably

Folegandros thrives on a small-scale tourism model, which already aligns well with sustainable travel principles. But there's always more we can do as conscientious travelers.

Embrace the slow travel ethos:

One of the island's greatest gifts is time. Rather than hopping from beach to beach, choose to stay longer in fewer places. Spend a week in Chora or settle into Ano Meria for a few days. This reduces transportation emissions and offers a deeper connection with the local community.

Support small businesses:

From family-run tavernas to artisans selling handmade jewelry and local honey, choosing where you spend your money can have a direct positive impact. Skip international chains and opt for locally owned accommodations and eateries.

Reduce your carbon footprint:

- Take the ferry instead of flying between islands when possible.
- Walk or take the island's efficient public bus to get around.
- If you rent a vehicle, opt for a scooter or an electric car (available through select services in high season).

Travel in the shoulder season:

May-June and September-October offer perfect weather with fewer crowds. This eases strain on resources and gives you a more authentic experience with locals who aren't rushed off their feet.

20.2 Eco-Friendly Tours & Lodging

As sustainability gains momentum across the Cyclades, Folegandros is quietly cultivating a network of eco-conscious experiences and stays. While you won't find five-star eco-resorts here, what you will discover is far more meaningful: places and people grounded in authenticity, simplicity, and respect for the environment.

Eco-conscious places to stay:

- **Provalma Studios (Ano Meria):** Built with locally sourced stone, this hillside retreat uses passive cooling, solar energy, and local products. It blends seamlessly into the landscape and offers expansive views without impacting the surroundings.

- **Anemi Hotel (Karavostasis):** While luxurious, Anemi makes efforts toward environmental responsibility through energy-efficient systems, native plant landscaping, and sustainable sourcing for its restaurant.

Sustainable activities:

- **Hiking the island's trails:** Folegandros boasts ancient mule paths and cliffside tracks that are ideal for low-impact exploration. Bring reusable water bottles and avoid straying off the trail to protect endemic flora.

- **Local cooking workshops:** These experiences support village economies and reduce food miles. Look for small-group classes in Chora or Ano Meria that use organic, local ingredients.

- **Boat tours with an ecological conscience:** Some operators, particularly those with smaller, solar-powered vessels, offer intimate excursions with a focus on marine conservation and education.

Tip: Always ask your host or tour provider about their sustainability efforts. The more travelers ask, the more businesses adapt.

20.3 Respecting Local Culture & Communities

Greek island culture is a mosaic of deep-rooted traditions, seasonal rhythms, and quiet pride. On Folegandros, where tourism hasn't overtaken daily life, visitors have a unique chance to participate, if they do so with humility and curiosity.

Cultural etiquette:

- Dress modestly when visiting churches or rural villages. Shoulders and knees should be covered, especially during religious festivals.

- Greet locals with a friendly "Kalimera" (good morning) or "Kalispera" (good evening). A smile goes a long way.

- Be mindful of noise, especially during siesta hours (2 p.m. to 5 p.m.), when many residents rest or retreat indoors.

Supporting traditional practices:

Many families still farm or raise animals using age-old methods. When you buy mizithra cheese, capers, or raki, ask where it's from. More often than not, it's from someone's grandmother's backyard. Purchasing these items sustains a way of life under threat from modernization.

Photography with respect:

- Always ask before taking pictures of people or private property.
- During religious processions or festivals, observe quietly unless invited to participate.

20.4 Waste Management & Water Use Tips

Folegandros has limited resources and a fragile infrastructure. Its dry, rocky landscape means that water is precious, and waste disposal is a logistical challenge. By making conscious choices, you help reduce strain on the island's ecosystem.

Minimizing waste:

- Carry a reusable water bottle. While tap water isn't potable, many hotels offer filtered options, and some stores have refill stations.

- Avoid single-use plastics. Bring reusable bags, cutlery, and containers for takeout or beach picnics.

- Recycle responsibly. Recycling bins for plastic, metal, and paper are available in Chora and Karavostasis, use them correctly.

Water conservation:

- Limit showers to a few minutes and turn off the tap while brushing your teeth.

- Reuse towels and linens during your stay instead of requesting daily changes.

- Be conscious of toilet flushing and laundry, especially if staying in a remote location where water must be transported in.

Beach and trail etiquette:

- Take all trash with you, even organic waste like fruit peels.

- Avoid using commercial sunscreens that harm marine life; opt for reef-safe formulas.

- Do not feed or disturb wildlife. Folegandros is home to rare birds and small reptiles that thrive best without human interference.

Travel with Heart, Leave Only Footprints

To travel responsibly on Folegandros is to engage deeply, with the land, with the people, and with the ancient rhythms that pulse beneath the modern façade. This is not a place that rewards the checklist tourist; it is a place that invites you to slow down, listen, and tread lightly.

Each choice we make as travelers has an impact. Will we stay in the family-owned guesthouse, where our euros support a child's education? Will we refill our bottles instead of tossing plastic into the wind? Will we hike with reverence, shop with care, and dine with gratitude?

I believe Folegandros rewards those who travel with intention. The island whispers her stories to those who pause long enough to hear them.

Chapter 21: For the Instagrammer & Photographer

There's something undeniably cinematic about Folegandros. Whether it's the sugar-cube houses clinging to dramatic cliffs, golden light spilling into stone alleyways at sunset, or the shimmer of the Aegean as it merges with cobalt skies, this island seduces the lens. Every corner holds a story. And for those of us who travel with a camera in hand or content on our mind, Folegandros delivers visual poetry in every frame.

As someone who has returned here time and again, drawn by the way this island seems to shift its expression with every season and shadow, I've come to know where the light lingers longest and where the colors sing their loudest. In this chapter, I'll share my favorite spots, timing secrets, and photography tips, along with how to share your work meaningfully with the world, without losing the authenticity that makes Folegandros so timeless.

21.1 Most Photogenic Spots on the Island

Folegandros isn't about flashy landmarks or mass-tourism icons, it's about composition, texture, and atmosphere. These are the island's most visually captivating locations, each with its own magic.

1. Chora at Sunset:

Perched on a cliff, the island's main village offers dreamy alleyways, whitewashed chapels, and vibrant bougainvillea. As the sun sinks behind the horizon, the marble lanes glow gold and pink. Don't miss photographing the Church of Panagia, especially from the zigzagging path below, it's the quintessential Folegandros shot.

2. The Church of Panagia (Panagía tis Koimíseos):

Dramatically set on a hill above Chora, this is arguably the most iconic viewpoint. Climb up at dusk for breathtaking panoramic shots over the island, with sea and sky stretching endlessly around you.

3. Kastro District:

The oldest part of Chora, Kastro, is a rabbit warren of medieval houses with arched passageways and pastel-painted doors. In early morning light, when shutters creak open and cats curl in doorways, the character of old Folegandros comes alive in every photo.

4. Agali Beach:

The view of Agali from the cliffs above, especially in early morning light or during the quieter shoulder seasons, captures the tranquil, aquamarine beauty of Folegandros's coastline. It's less crowded and more serene than other beach spots, and its natural curves frame perfectly in wide-angle shots.

5. Livadaki Beach:

Only accessible by foot or boat, Livadaki is the hidden gem every photographer dreams of. Think of bleached pebbles, aquamarine shallows, and dramatic rock faces. The effort to get there pays off in untouched, postcard-worthy images.

6. Ano Meria's Terraces & Windmills:
For rural charm and textural storytelling, this village in the north is a treasure. Photograph traditional agricultural terraces, half-crumbled windmills, and goats silhouetted against the morning sky. It's the Folegandros of another century.

21.2 Best Time of Day for Lighting & Crowds

In photography, timing isn't just everything, it's the difference between a snapshot and a masterpiece.

Golden Hour (Sunrise & Sunset):
The first light of day brings a quiet stillness to Chora and the beaches. It's when colors soften, shadows stretch, and the village slowly comes to life. For portraits or atmospheric shots, this hour is unbeatable. Similarly, the late afternoon golden hour, especially from the Panagia path or above Karavostasis, bathes the island in warmth and romance.

Blue Hour (Dusk):

Just after sunset, the sky turns to rich navy and the village lights begin to twinkle. Shoot from the upper path above Chora or down at the port, long exposures during blue hour can create dramatic, moody scenes.

Midday (For Colors):

Though often harsh, the midday light in Folegandros makes colors pop. It's perfect for shooting architecture, the vibrancy of flowers, or capturing contrast against a blazing blue sky. Use a polarizing filter for deeper hues.

Avoid Peak Midday at Crowded Spots: From late June through August, avoid shooting major landmarks between 11 a.m. and 3 p.m., unless you want crowded compositions. Instead, head to quieter corners or beaches like Vardia or Ambeli for clean, undisturbed shots.

21.3 Local Photographers & Workshops

If you're looking to deepen your craft while in Folegandros, consider connecting with local creatives. The island might be small, but it boasts a growing community of photographers and visual storytellers who intimately understand how to capture its soul.

Recommended Photographers & Experiences:

- **Yannis Markopoulos (based seasonally in Chora):** Known for his hauntingly beautiful landscape photography, Yannis occasionally offers private photo walks focusing on light, composition, and storytelling in traditional villages.

- **Workshops with Cycladic Light Collective:** This small, eco-conscious photography group hosts seasonal workshops in the Cyclades, often including Folegandros as a destination. Their retreats combine technical training with cultural immersion.

Photography Walks:

Some boutique hotels, like Blue Sand Boutique Hotel & Suites, partner with local artists to offer curated photo tours, often starting at dawn or ending at sunset.

Tip: Whether joining a workshop or walking solo, always ask permission before photographing residents, especially in smaller villages where life remains deeply private.

21.4 Top Hashtags & Social Media Tips

Let's be honest: if you've traveled all this way, you'll want to share the magic. But social media can do more than showcase your travel aesthetic, it can inspire others to travel responsibly, support local businesses, and explore beyond the obvious.

Top Instagram-Worthy Hashtags:

- #Folegandros
- #FolegandrosIsland
- #CycladesDiaries
- #GreekIslandHopping
- #SecretCyclades
- #VisitGreece
- #ChoraFolegandros
- #PanagiaView

Mix popular tags with niche ones for a balanced reach. Tag local businesses too, many, like cafes and guesthouses, will often reshare and feature your content.

Smart Sharing Tips:

- **Geotag thoughtfully.** If a spot is particularly secluded or vulnerable, consider tagging the general area rather than the exact location to preserve its charm.

- **Caption with context.** A short story about your experience can be more engaging than a simple description.

- **Engage with the community.** Follow local creators and interact with fellow travelers using the same hashtags, and you'll find inspiration and maybe even new friendships.

Seeing with More than the Lens

Photographing Folegandros is not about checking off famous landmarks. It's about learning to see, really see, the textures, the shadows, the quiet stories etched into every stone wall and every salt-worn door.

The most rewarding images, in my experience, aren't the ones that go viral. They're the ones that bring you back to a moment of stillness, a smile exchanged with a shopkeeper, the way the wind tousled your hair as the church bells rang above Chora.

So bring your camera, your phone, your drone if you must, but above all, bring your eye for wonder. Let Folegandros show you how light dances, how color speaks, how silence can be its own kind of music.

And if you share it with the world, do it with heart. Because this island, with its unfiltered beauty and deep soul, deserves to be captured with care, and remembered with reverence.

Chapter 22: What Not to Do in Folegandros

A Traveler's Cautionary Tale: Navigating the Island with Respect, Wisdom, and Wonder

I've seen it all, the first-timers who arrived with high hopes and the wrong shoes, the Instagrammers chasing sunsets while missing the soul of the village, and the enthusiastic travelers who stumbled, quite innocently, into local faux pas. Folegandros, for all its serenity and charm, is not your typical tourist playground. It's a place that rewards the curious and respectful while quietly resisting the careless and entitled.

This chapter is your travel insurance in words, a lovingly honest guide to what not to do on this stunning Cycladic island. I don't say this to scare you off, but rather to make your journey smoother, more meaningful, and infinitely more rewarding.

22.1 Common Mistakes First-Time Visitors Make

Even the most seasoned globe-trotter can misstep when exploring new terrain. Folegandros, with its unique rhythm and raw beauty, demands a little forethought.

1. Rushing the Experience:

Folegandros is not an island you conquer with a checklist. It's meant to be lived, not "done." I've watched people breeze through in 24 hours, tick off Chora and the Church of Panagia, and leave having missed the island's essence. This isn't Santorini, there are no busloads of tourists here (yet), and that's exactly the point.

2. Assuming Easy Access Everywhere:

While charmingly compact, Folegandros is rugged. Some of the most beautiful beaches, like Livadaki or Katergo, require boat rides or challenging hikes. Flip-flops won't cut it. Bring sturdy walking shoes, water, and sun protection for any off-road adventure.

3. Underestimating the Wind:

Folegandros is famously breezy. The meltemi, a fierce northern wind that can howl during summer months, often surprises visitors. It can disrupt ferry schedules, beach plans, and even a well-planned photo shoot. Always have a flexible itinerary and check local forecasts.

4. Not Booking Accommodation in Advance (Especially in August):

The island remains delightfully uncrowded compared to Mykonos or Paros, but it's still wise to plan ahead. During peak months, especially in August when Athenians flock to the Cyclades, charming boutique hotels and local guesthouses fill up fast.

22.2 What's Considered Rude or Taboo

Folegandros may be welcoming, but like any place rooted in tradition, it comes with its own cultural nuances. Understanding what not to say or do is just as important as knowing where to go.

1. Being Loud and Disruptive in Chora:
The quiet streets of Chora are more than postcard material, they're home. Life moves gently here. Loud voices, booming Bluetooth speakers, or raucous behavior disrupt the very peace that makes this village special. Speak softly, especially at night.

2. Ignoring Church Etiquette:
There are over 60 chapels on the island, each a spiritual landmark. When visiting churches, dress modestly, cover shoulders and knees, and refrain from taking photos during services. Even outside of religious events, locals appreciate reverence over selfies.

3. Pointing Your Feet Toward Icons or Altars:
In Greek Orthodox culture, pointing your feet toward religious icons (or sitting with them facing a church interior) is considered deeply disrespectful. A small thing, but worth remembering if you're resting on church steps or exploring inside.

4. Taking Photos of Locals Without Permission: Especially in Ano Meria and older parts of Chora, you'll encounter long-time residents tending gardens, chatting in courtyards, or riding donkeys. Don't photograph them without asking, it's a matter of dignity and mutual respect.

22.3 Overhyped Spots vs. Genuine Experiences

Instagram and travel blogs tend to spotlight the same few frames: the path to the Church of Panagia, the cliffside cafes in Chora, and the boats anchored in Agali Bay. They're beautiful, no doubt, but there's so much more to Folegandros than these social media stars.

Skip the Sunset Scramble at the Church (Some Nights): Yes, the view is magical, but everyone knows it. Instead of elbowing your way to the edge of the cliff, find a terrace cafe in Chora with a westward view. I recommend Pounta Cafe, order a rakomelo and watch the show in peace.

Seek Out Hidden Taverns in Ano Meria: While Chora's restaurants get the spotlight, Ano Meria's traditional tavernas, like To Zimaraki, offer deeply authentic, hyper-local food. Think homemade matsata (handmade pasta), stewed goat, and sweet watermelon preserves.

Trade Crowded Beaches for Solitude:
Instead of heading straight to Agios Nikolaos (which can be busy in summer), take the cliff path down to Fira Beach or ask a fisherman in Karavostasis to drop you at Voreina. These offbeat beaches are the kind of hidden paradise you'll remember forever.

22.4 Weather Hazards & Travel Miscalculations

The weather on Folegandros can be as dramatic as its cliffs, and those unaware may find their plans literally blown away.

1. The Ferocious Meltemi Wind:
From late June to early September, the northern meltemi winds whip across the island. They can make boat excursions impossible and walking along cliff paths uncomfortable or dangerous. If you're planning a day trip or hike, always check conditions with your host or the local weather center.

2. Summer Heat Deceit:
The breeze can make summer temperatures feel cooler than they are, which leads to unintentional overexposure. Sunscreen, hats, and hydration are a must, even on windier days.

3. Ferry Cancellations and Delays:
Folegandros is linked to the Cyclades by sea, and during windy spells or off-season months, ferries can be delayed or canceled entirely.

Build in buffer days before and after your trip to accommodate travel disruptions, especially if you have international flights.

4. Underestimating Hiking Trails:
The hiking paths in Folegandros are stunning but rarely shaded. Many are unmarked and rocky. It's easy to get sunburned, disoriented, or dehydrated. Avoid hiking during the hottest hours, bring ample water, and download offline maps or carry a trail guide.

Travel with Intention, Leave with Meaning

There's an intimacy to Folegandros, a quiet, breathless beauty that doesn't need embellishment. But to receive it fully, you must approach with intention. This is not the island for ticking boxes or following influencers. It's for those who want to wander slowly, to listen, to taste what's real.

Avoid the common pitfalls, observe the unspoken rules, and resist the temptation to force an experience. In doing so, you'll open yourself to the kind of travel that lingers in your bones long after the ferry has pulled away. And perhaps, like me, you'll find yourself coming back, not to see more, but to feel it all again.

Chapter 23: Final Departure Tips

A Gentle Goodbye to Folegandros: What to Know Before You Go

There's a particular melancholy in leaving a place like Folegandros. The island lingers in your senses, the scent of wild thyme on the wind, the salty kiss of the Aegean on sun-warmed skin, the echo of goat bells drifting across terraced hills. I've said goodbye to Folegandros more times than I'd like to admit, and every time, it's as if the island presses a fingerprint on my soul. But departures, like arrivals, are part of the journey. This chapter is for that final stretch: when your heart is full, your suitcase is nearly overflowing, and you're not quite ready to say farewell.

23.1 How to Get Back (Ferries, Transfers, Flights)

Leaving Folegandros can be logistically smooth if planned properly. Though the island feels like a secluded paradise, it's well-connected, if you know the ropes.

Ferries: Your Main Escape Route

Most travelers leave Folegandros by ferry, and I always recommend booking your return journey as early as possible, especially during high season (June to September). Ferries depart from Karavostasis Port, and services connect to Santorini, Milos, Naxos, Paros, and Piraeus (Athens).

- **High-Speed Ferries:** These are faster but often more sensitive to weather, especially during strong meltemi winds. They're ideal if you're trying to reach Santorini or Milos quickly.

- **Conventional Ferries:** Slower, larger, and generally more stable in rough conditions, perfect for a relaxed, scenic journey.

Pro Tip: Always double-check ferry times 24 hours before your departure. Schedules can change due to weather or port logistics. If you're leaving from Chora, allow at least 30 minutes to drive down to the port and another 20 minutes for boarding.

Transfers & Local Transport

There are no taxis queuing at the port like in larger islands, so pre-arranged transfers are essential. Many hotels offer shuttle services to the port, often timed with major ferry departures. If you're renting a car or scooter, arrange to drop it off at the port, many rental agencies in Chora or Karavostasis will accommodate this.

Flights from Nearby Islands

Folegandros doesn't have its own airport, so you'll need to fly out of Santorini (JTR) or Milos (MLO). I personally prefer Santorini for international connections, but Milos is a quieter alternative for domestic flights.

- From **Folegandros to Santorini**: 40-minute fast ferry
- From **Folegandros to Milos**: 1.5-hour fast ferry

Tip for International Travelers: Always allow for ferry delays. If you're flying internationally, spend a night on the departure island to buffer against any disruptions. Santorini, with its bustling nightlife and endless views, makes for a poetic last stop.

23.2 Last-Minute Gift & Souvenir Guide

If you're anything like me, your suitcase might already be bulging with woven textiles, sun hats, and jars of capers. But if you've waited until the end to shop for souvenirs, fear not, Folegandros has plenty of locally made treasures that capture the island's essence.

Where to Shop

- **Chora's Boutique Alleyways:** The labyrinthine lanes of Chora are dotted with charming shops and artisan studios. My favorite haunt is To Spitiko Tou Nikou, a family-run store with handmade ceramics, embroidered linens, and herbal sachets.

- **Ano Meria Agricultural Co-op:** For something truly authentic, visit the rural cooperative in Ano Meria. They sell locally made rakomelo, jars of wild thyme honey, dried figs, and sousoura, a fig-based digestif you won't find elsewhere.

Gift Ideas That Travel Well:

- **Hand-embroidered textiles** – Table runners, pillowcases, and napkins
- **Sea salt & herbs** – Locally harvested from rocky cliffs
- **Homemade preserves** – Watermelon, fig, and tomato jam
- **Goat's milk soap** – Scented with lavender or olive oil
- **Artisanal jewelry** – Often made from sea glass and volcanic stone

If you've visited during one of the island's panigiria (festivals), you may have picked up handmade trinkets or even woven baskets crafted by local women. These make heartfelt gifts with a story.

Don't forget: Liquids over 100ml aren't allowed in carry-on bags, so pack larger bottles of rakomelo or olive oil in checked luggage.

23.3 Ending Your Trip Gracefully: What to Remember

The final day of your trip deserves care and attention. It's a time to reflect, to close the loop on your experience, and to say a proper goodbye, not only to the island but to the version of yourself that emerged while you were here.

Slow Down One Last Time

Instead of rushing to pack, I always recommend starting your last day with one final coffee in the square at Piazza Café. Watch the whitewashed houses turn gold in the morning sun, listen to the locals exchange news, and take in that sacred Folegandros quietude one more time.

A Farewell Meal

Before departure, treat yourself to a leisurely lunch or dinner. Irini's Restaurant in Ano Meria serves some of the best slow-cooked lamb on the island. Or dine by the sea in Karavostasis at Syrma, where fresh grilled fish and a final glass of assyrtiko make for a perfect culinary send-off.

Packing Tips for the Way Out:

- Double-bag liquids to prevent spills.
- Wrap fragile items like ceramics in clothing.
- Carry a small tote with essentials (snacks, chargers, water, ferry tickets).

Leave a Little Piece of Gratitude

One tradition I love is leaving behind a small note, tucked under a guesthouse pillow, written in a visitor's book, or handed to a shopkeeper who made your day. Folegandros is shaped by the people who live here, and your words of thanks ripple through the community more than you might imagine.

Stay Connected, but Let Go Too

Yes, post your best sunset photo, tag the taverna that fed you soulfully, and follow the local artist you met in Chora. But also give yourself space to hold parts of the journey offline. Some memories belong to the heart, not the algorithm.

Parting with Presence

Departures can feel abrupt, like waking from a dream. But Folegandros isn't a dream you wake from; it's one you carry with you. Whether it's the sight of fishing boats bobbing in Karavostasis, the way the stars fall over Chora's rooftops, or the taste of wild figs bursting in your mouth, the island stays.

As you ferry away, watch the cliffs recede into blue, not with sadness but with gratitude. You came as a visitor. You leave as a quiet witness to something ancient, simple, and enduring.

And if you're anything like me, you'll come back, not just for the views, but for the peace they gave you.

The journey doesn't end here, it simply changes shape.

Until next time, kalo taxidi.

Chapter 24: Appendices & Bonus Resources

A Practical Traveler's Toolkit for Exploring Folegandros with Confidence and Curiosity

Traveling to Folegandros is more than just wandering sunlit alleys or lounging beside aquamarine coves, it's about feeling prepared, empowered, and attuned to the rhythms of island life. This chapter is your toolkit. It's not just a repository of logistical facts; it's the distilled wisdom of years spent exploring this Aegean gem, capturing sunsets, sharing laughs over rakomelo, and navigating ferry strikes with grace and a pinch of patience.

So, before you zip up your suitcase or step aboard a ferry, take this section as your compass. It will guide you through the Greek phrases you'll wish you knew, the festivals you don't want to miss, the blogs worth bookmarking, and the numbers you'll be glad to have at your fingertips.

24.1 Essential Greek Phrases for Travelers

Even a few words in Greek can open doors and hearts. While most locals speak English, especially in hospitality, your effort to speak the language is always met with appreciation.

Here are the essentials I use often:

- **Kalimera** – Good morning
- **Kalispera** – Good evening
- **Efcharistó** – Thank you
- **Parakaló** – Please / You're welcome
- **Signómi** – Excuse me / Sorry
- **Poso kostízei?** – How much does it cost?
- **Pou einai to limani?** – Where is the port?
- **Neró, parakaló.** – Water, please.
- **To logariasmó, parakaló.** – The bill, please.
- **Miláte Angliká?** – Do you speak English?

Tip: Learn how to say thank you with a smile, "Efcharistó!", and you'll leave a warm impression wherever you go.

24.2 Travel Resources: Sites, Books & Blogs

Over the years, I've found that the best travel experience is equal parts spontaneity and research. These are the resources I return to time and again:

Websites

- https://www.greeka.com – Great for ferry schedules, island insights, and accommodation reviews.
- https://www.gtp.gr – Greek Travel Pages, a reliable source for transportation timetables.
- https://www.visitgreece.gr – Official Greek tourism site for events and general info.

Books

- "The Rough Guide to the Greek Islands" – A handy companion for broader Aegean travel.
- "Greek Islands" by Lawrence Durrell – Evocative prose that'll deepen your appreciation of island culture.
- "Blue Guide Greece" – For art and archaeology buffs wanting rich historical context.

Blogs & Digital Guides

- My Greece Travel Blog – First-hand stories and seasonal updates.
- Santorini Dave – Offers insights into ferry routes and hotel recommendations.

- Folegandros Lovers (Facebook Group) – A community of fellow fans sharing tips and updates.

24.3 Contact Info: Tourism Office, Police, Hospitals

In case of emergencies or if you need quick assistance, here are the key contacts to keep handy:

- **Folegandros Tourist Information Office**
  Chora, Main Square
  +30 22860 41285

- **Police Station (Astynomia)**
  Karavostasis
  +30 22860 41249

- **Medical Center (Kentro Ygeias Folegandrou)**
  Chora
  +30 22860 41214
  Open 24 hours for basic care and emergencies.

- **Fire Department (for wildfires or accidents)**
  +30 22860 41299

Tip: Save these contacts in your phone before you arrive, along with your embassy's number if traveling internationally.

24.4 Important Addresses & GPS Links

Navigating Folegandros is mostly intuitive; there's no labyrinth like in Santorini or Mykonos, but a few GPS markers can save time and stress.

Karavostasis Port (Ferry Terminal)

Google Maps Link

Chora Central Square (Piazza Café)

Google Maps Link

Christos Church (Sunset Spot)

Google Maps Link

Ano Meria Folklore Museum

Google Maps Link

Taxi & Shuttle Stand (Karavostasis)

Google Maps Link

Tip: Download offline maps of the island using Google Maps or Maps.me, cell service can be spotty in remote areas like Livadaki beach or behind the cliffs of Agios Nikolaos.

24.5 Festival Calendar & Local Events

Folegandros, while serene and small, holds deeply rooted traditions that shine brightest during local festivals. The festivals, panigiria, are spirited, authentic, and celebratory, drawing the entire community together in joyful communion.

Key Events to Watch For:

- **July 20 – Feast of Prophet Elias**
  Celebrated with a procession to the chapel on the hill, live music, and a sunset meal.

- **August 15 – Assumption of the Virgin Mary (Dekapentavgoustos)**
  The biggest celebration of the year. Expect music, dancing, lamb feasts, and moonlit revelry in Chora.

- **Late September – Harvest Festival**
  An intimate event in Ano Meria celebrating local food, particularly figs, grapes, and herbs.

Many panigiria include traditional instruments like the tsambouna (Greek bagpipe) and spontaneous dancing. Don't be shy, locals will gladly show you the steps.

24.6 Packing Checklist Travel Journal Pages

Packing Checklist (Island Edition):

- Lightweight layers + swimsuit
- Reef-safe sunscreen
- Walking shoes + sandals
- Power bank + travel adapter
- Snorkel gear (if desired)
- Ferry tickets (paper or digital)

Travel Journal Prompts:

- "What was your favorite beach and why?"
- "Describe the best meal you had."
- "Which moment made you feel most connected to the island?"
- "What will you bring back, not in your suitcase, but in your heart?"

24.7 Local Ferry Schedules & Transportation Contacts

Folegandros' ferry network is seasonal and ever-changing, so flexibility is key. Below is a general overview, but always confirm schedules with the operator or via https://www.openseas.gr.

Summer Routes (June–September):

- **Santorini ↔ Folegandros** – Daily (SeaJets, Zante Ferries)
- **Milos ↔ Folegandros** – 3-4 times/week
- **Naxos ↔ Folegandros** – 2-3 times/week

Main Ferry Operators:

- **SeaJets:** +30 210 710 7710 | https://www.seajets.gr
- **Zante Ferries:** +30 210 410 0211 | https://www.zanteferries.gr
- **Golden Star Ferries:** https://www.goldenstarferries.gr

Local Transport Providers:

- **Taxi (Stavros):** +30 697 414 8052
- **Island Shuttle (Hotel Transfers):** Pre-book with your hotel
- **Car/Scooter Rentals:** Try Chora Moto or Folegandros Rent-a-Car

The Details That Make a Difference

Sometimes it's the little things, the right phrase, a trusted phone number, knowing that a festival is just around the corner, that turn a good trip into a great one. This chapter isn't glamorous, but it's your safety net, your cheat sheet, your local whisperer in written form.

When you're sitting at a seaside taverna, waiting for your ferry with a glass of ouzo in hand and the island breeze at your back, you'll know: you came prepared, and it made all the difference.

And if Folegandros has worked its quiet magic on you, as it has on me, then maybe, just maybe, this won't be your last time on its shores.

Save these pages. You'll want them again.

Printed in Dunstable, United Kingdom

69187953R00107